Test Your Trivia I.Q.

Test Your Trivia I.Q.

By Loreen Arbus

A Perigee Book

Perigee Books
are published by
The Putnam Publishing Group
200 Madison Avenue
New York, NY 10016

Library of Congress Cataloging in Publication Data

Arbus, Loreen, date.
Test your trivia IQ.

"Perigee books."
Summary: Asks and answers such trivial questions as
"What is the longest running television series in the
U.S.?" and "In what country did the croissant originate?"
("Meet the Press"; Austria)
1. Questions and answers.   [1. Questions and answers.
2. Trivial Pursuit (Game)]   I. Title.
AG195.A777 1984   031'.02   84-6961
ISBN 0-399-51098-2

Printed in the United States of America
1 2 3 4 5 6 7 8 9 10

Acknowledgments

Big, big thanks to Jack Artenstein, who made possible my first book. Extra special thanks to Gene Brissie, who bought my first book, always has answers to endless questions, and is good-natured and helpful at any hour, but should be sainted for the way he handles midnight calls and weekend obtrusions. Gratitude to Ira Ritter, emperor of media moguldom and wonderful friend. No bill, no matter how trivial, could assay the meticulousness, alacrity, genuine interest, and incomparable style of my attorney, Susan Grode. My appreciation to the management of Viacom for always supporting my efforts to realize my potential. Finally, thanks from the heart to my overqualified, bonified brilliant assistant, Lindsay Smith, who is there for me. These people score 100% because—they are.

A grillion thanks to my Associate Researchers, trivia buffs all:

1. Robert Rogers, who spent five weeks at MGM doing factual/historical research on 150 motion pictures, 62 Movies of the Week, and 52 TV series . . . known by friends far and wide as "Mr. Correctness."

2. Clyde Derrick, who was born on Friday the 13th, at the age of 12 wrote to 25 pen pals in Great Britain, saw his first ghost at the age of 20, and whose paternal great-grandparents met as prospectors in the Alaska Gold Rush of 1898.

3. Valerie Hoffman, who has traveled from Ibiza to Iraklion to Ashkelon, owns 23 Nina Simone albums, co-authored *The Art of the Empire Strikes Back,* and currently experiments with raku pottery.

4. Jeanne Feder, who before becoming a television toiler used to paint and sell paintings under the name Harold Smiley.

5. Julie Resh, who at three jumped into Robert Young's lap in a restaurant; at fourteen was thrown into jail in Florence—falsely accused of trying to sell her passport.

6. Dana Hood, who was born in St. Louis, but plans never to return there, has a pink cat, a Harvard-educated husband and a divine daughter named Kate.

7. Paul Morgan, who spent four years with the U.S. Navy, during which time he read extensively from the collected works of Walt Kelly and fired over 50,000 rounds of 5″ ammunition—none in anger.

8. Dennis Gutierrez, who worked for Carl Sagan as a production assistant on *Cosmos* and got to travel cross-country for free—it was the first time in his life that he'd been east of Carlsbad, New Mexico.

9. Nancy Fawcett, a twin, who was in the peanut gallery of *The Howdy Doody Show,* and is the granddaughter of the inventor of the round-doored safe.

10. Art Goldsher, who, once upon a time, was an extra in *Annie Hall.*

11. Kim Wells, born September 16—Mexican Independence Day—which may explain her fondness for margueritas; since leaving her native Canada has worked extensively with financial concerns—without ever learning to balance her own checkbook.

12. Janet Renee Brown, who once upon a New York day in time, looked into most peaceful eyes . . . only when the light had changed and the crowd exclaimed . . . did she realize she had just shared a moment with John Lennon?

13. Michael Artenstein, who while in Denmark at a dinner given in his honor, tried to impress all present by heroically lighting the cigarette of a lady across the table—and inadvertently set his arm on fire.

For Norm
Who conceived this book with me;
Whose ideas, generosity, and energy provided nourishment
     during its gestation; and
Who joyously shared in its rapid-fire birth—
   With eternal love from your best friend and
   soulmate,

                                              L.J.A.

Contents

Introduction

Do *You* Know Your T.I.Q.?

Everybody is talking about trivia! The warehouse of factual odds and ends between our ears is categorized as trivia. Webster defines "trivia" as "unimportant matters or trifles." However, the sum total of assorted *facts* is . . . KNOWLEDGE! By the conclusion of this book, you will probably have discovered how surprisingly well you retrieve little-used bits of information that have been relegated to a back-of-the-brain file room. The amazing thing is that most of us don't realize how much unused information we store in those dusty vaults. How much trivia do *you* know?

Now, for the first time, *you* can actually *rate* your trivia intelligence quotient. This trivia intelligence quotient, henceforth known as your "T.I.Q.," gives you an index or numerical handle on what you know in various subjects. Best of all, you'll ascertain the areas of trivia knowledge in which you're strongest and which areas need improvement. For those of you who may be a little insecure about playing trivia games, you have the opportunity to take some trial runs to evaluate how good you are and to hone your skills. If you're a trivia game veteran, you can increase your self-confidence and pride by seeing how you rate against others. Most importantly for old and new trivia buffs is the fact that you can easily assimilate vast quantities of information just by repeating the tests.

Trivia games are sweeping the country. Trivia champions are competing in national tournaments. In fact, trivia is becoming a social by-word with friends gathering at numerous parties just for the purpose of playing trivia games.

Mastering trivia can be extraordinarily meaningful. Spouting a snippet of trivia can spark a long conversation with someone you've been wanting to meet and impress. Learning an interesting fact about someone or something may open up whole new areas of personal or professional interest to you. While you may be an expert in one field, just think how rewarding it can be to know useful information about many areas. The added bonus is that you can hold your own with trivia game competitors.

The purpose of the six tests in this book is two-fold: have fun and *increase* your T.I.Q. When you look up the answers, which are at the end of each chapter, you'll also find a brief amplification of the answer, which is designed to help you remember the fact.

The six tests are in the following areas: General Information, Science, History, Entertainment, The Arts, and Sports. You can take the tests as they appear in the order of the book, or you can select the area that interests you the most and later take on the subjects with which you are least familiar. I suggest that you write your test answers—just the number of the question and the letters a, b, c, or d—on a *separate* piece of paper rather than in the book. Because you'll want to improve your scores, it's important eventually to take *all* the tests a number of times in order to broaden your horizons. You may even find that your least favorite subject becomes a consuming passion.

Carry this book with you to learn some interesting facts while you're waiting in line at the bank or the grocery store checkout. Turn tedious train, air, or bus trips into voyages of self-improvement. Quiz your friends, lover, classmates or co-workers—and particularly that acquaintance who claims to be an expert on everything.

The exams are about to begin. Your T.I.Q. has nowhere to go but *up!* Have fun!

ONE

General Information

(Geography, Food, Wine, Business, Products, Money, Travel)

1. Which is the holiest city in Islam?
   a. Medina
   b. Mecca
   c. Islamabad
   d. Cairo

2. What grain product is the traditional dish of North Africa?
   a. Pilaf
   b. Tabouli
   c. Tahini
   d. Couscous

3. How many months out of the year does the average taxpayer work just to pay his taxes?
   a. Six
   b. Eight
   c. Four
   d. Two

4. The Pennines is a small mountain range in which country?
   a. Ireland
   b. England
   c. Australia
   d. Canada

5. What Chinese snack is eaten as a "tea lunch"?
   a. Dim Sum
   b. Won Ton
   c. Almond cakes
   d. Mongolian Hot Pot

6. Who was the first man to introduce a breakfast cereal?
   a. James Kellogg
   b. Bernard McFadden
   c. Thomas Meecham
   d. William Post

7. In what picturesque Austrian city was Mozart born?
   a. Linz
   b. Salzburg
   c. Innsbruck
   d. Vienna

8. Bourbon is distilled primarily from which grain?
   a. Wheat
   b. Barley
   c. Corn
   d. Rice

9. Who started the first five-and-dime store?
   a. Elias Roebuck
   b. Daniel Webster
   c. Frank Woolworth
   d. Barbara Hutton

10. Which state has the country's highest rate of alcoholism?
    a. New York
    b. California
    c. Illinois
    d. Nevada

11. What Chinese delicacy is buried for two to four months before it is eaten?
    a. Thousand-year-old eggs
    b. Huo Kuo
    c. Beggar's Chicken
    d. Cha Shao Bao

12. What was the name of the company that ran rhyming billboards along the highways?
    a. Gillette
    b. Ipana
    c. Burma Shave
    d. Schick

13. In which state can one find London Bridge?
    a. Texas
    b. Florida
    c. Connecticut
    d. Arizona

14. What phrase originally meant that cognac had not been darkened with additives?
    a. RSVP
    b. Cuvée Speciale
    c. VSOP
    d. Neutral spirits

15. What company sponsored the very first television commercial?
    a. General Foods
    b. Procter & Gamble
    c. Bulova
    d. Lever Brothers

16. What city would you find the Hermitage Museum in?
    a. Amsterdam
    b. Leningrad
    c. Madrid
    d. Helsinki

17. What grape is used to make red Burgundy wine?
    a. Tokay
    b. Nebbiolo
    c. Merlot
    d. Pinot Noir

18. Who designed the Volkswagen bug?
    a. Emilio Bugatti
    b. Dr. Frederick Porsche
    c. Gerd Karmann
    d. Luigi Ghia

19. Which state is the grave of Martin Luther King in?
    a. Georgia
    b. Alabama
    c. Maryland
    d. Mississippi

20. What vegetable is the national emblem of Wales?
    a. Turnip
    b. Potato
    c. Leek
    d. Cabbage

21. Who invented the Bowie knife?
    a. James Bowie
    b. David Bowie
    c. Rezin Bowie
    d. Harry Hoffritz

22. Which state is Bryce Canyon National Park in?
    a. Arizona
    b. Utah
    c. Colorado
    d. Wyoming

23. What country produces the most wine in the world?
    a. Italy
    b. France
    c. Germany
    d. Spain

24. What product was Burt Reynolds smuggling in the film *Smokey and the Bandit*?
    a. Kent cigarettes
    b. Jack Daniel's whiskey
    c. Coors beer
    d. M & M candies

25. Where would you find the ruins of the Temple of Karnak?
    a. Greece
    b. Turkey
    c. Peru
    d. Egypt

26. What nut is used to make marzipan?
    a. Pecan
    b. Almond
    c. Walnut
    d. Chestnut

27. What popular product did Edwin Land invent?
    a. Microwave oven
    b. Automatic garage door
    c. Polaroid camera
    d. Zipper

28. What is the name of the country that was formerly called British Honduras?
    a. Bhutan
    b. Honduras
    c. Surinam
    d. Belize

29. What food product is made from the extract of boiled beef and bones?
    a. Gelatin
    b. Agar
    c. Arrowroot
    d. Wasabi

30. What's the reason that the Merchant's Coffee Shop is famous?
    a. Site of Madison Square Garden
    b. Site of Fulton Fish Market
    c. The New York Stock Exchange was formed there
    d. Site of the first commodity exchange in the U.S.

31. The ancient city of Troy was located in what country?
    a. Greece
    b. Egypt
    c. Cyprus
    d. Turkey

32. Who made the first chocolate chip cookie?
    a. James Beard
    b. Fannie Farmer
    c. Ruth Wakefield
    d. Irma Rombauer

33. Who was the first person to wear a wristwatch?
    a. George Washington
    b. Marco Polo
    c. Louis XIV
    d. Queen Elizabeth I

34. Which country is the kingdom of Hunza in?
    a. U.S.S.R.
    b. Pakistan
    c. China
    d. Nepal

35. What popular food was once thought to be a temptation of the devil?
    a. Sugar
    b. Peanuts
    c. Popcorn
    d. Chocolate

36. What's the largest chain of retail stores?
    a. Sears
    b. Macy's
    c. Montgomery Ward
    d. Woolworth's

37. Name the group of islands located to the east of the coast of Kenya.
    a. Solomon Islands
    b. Seychelles
    c. Azores
    d. Malvinas

38. Who were the world's first coffee drinkers?
    a. The Greeks
    b. The Italians
    c. The Viennese
    d. The Arabs

39. Which state is Three Mile Island in?
    a. New York
    b. Pennsylvania
    c. Maryland
    d. West Virginia

40. What was the name of the British colony of the Gold Coast called when it became independent?
    a. Togo
    b. Zaire
    c. Ghana
    d. Burundi

41. What food in the lily family is reputed to have magical powers?
    a. Leek
    b. Garlic
    c. Onion
    d. Shallot

42. What are the most frequent over-the-counter purchases in U.S. drugstores?
    a. Cough and cold remedies
    b. Aspirin
    c. Analgesics
    d. Antacids

43. What is spelunking?
    a. Rock climbing
    b. Digging for gold
    c. Cave exploration
    d. Rock collecting

44. What is the most varied and widespread staple food of human invention?
    a. Noodles
    b. Bread
    c. Pancakes
    d. Soup

45. Which state produces the most livestock?
    a. Oklahoma
    b. Iowa
    c. Texas
    d. Kansas

46. What name is given to the group of over 2500 islands scattered between Hawaii and the Philippines?
    a. Indonesia
    b. Micronesia
    c. Falkland Islands
    d. Azores

47. What well-known gourmet who now lives in the U.S. was once chef to Charles de Gaulle?
    a. Julia Child
    b. Louisette Bertholle
    c. Pierre Franey
    d. Graham Kerr

48. What shape is the tombstone of Gail Borden, the founder of Borden's?
    a. Cow
    b. Milk bottle
    c. Swiss cheese
    d. Can of condensed milk

49. What country is Lake Titicaca in?
    a. Peru
    b. Chile
    c. Guatemala
    d. Paraguay

50. Which restauranteur is credited with spawning the French restaurant revolution in America?
    a. Stewart Levine
    b. George Lang
    c. Henri Soulé
    d. Charles Masson

51. What was the original use of Coca-Cola?
    a. Iron tonic
    b. Headache remedy
    c. Hangover cure
    d. Antacid

52. Name the northernmost of the Hawaiian Islands.
    a. Maui
    b. Oahu
    c. Kauai
    d. Hawaii

53. What old English dish was often served when a hunter came home empty-handed?
    a. Trifle
    b. Yorkshire pudding
    c. Bubble and Squeak
    d. Welsh rabbit

54. For whom was the Baby Ruth candy bar named?
    a. Baseball player
    b. Ruth Cleveland
    c. Ruth from the Old Testament
    d. Babe Didrikson

55. Which city is the capital of Uganda?
    a. Khartoum
    b. Dakar
    c. Kampala
    d. Salisbury

56. Which American chef popularized French cooking for home use?
    a. James Beard
    b. Julia Child
    c. Michael Field
    d. Dione Lucas

57. What is the most purchased shoe in America?
    a. Tennis shoe
    b. Jogging shoe
    c. Loafer
    d. Boot

58. The San Juan Islands are on the border of what state?
    a. Florida
    b. Maine
    c. Michigan
    d. Washington

59. Two Roman restaurants with the same name both lay claim to what popular pasta dish?
    a. Lasagna
    b. Gnocchi
    c. Fettucine
    d. Mostaccioli

60. What American university has the most money?
    a. Yale
    b. Princeton
    c. Harvard
    d. Stanford

61. In what country is the famous spa of Baden-Baden located?
    a. Germany
    b. Czechoslovakia
    c. Switzerland
    d. Austria

62. What U.S. government body has a dish named after it?
    a. Supreme Court
    b. House of Representatives
    c. U.S. Senate
    d. Library of Congress

63. Name the tallest building in the United States.
    a. Empire State Building in New York City
    b. Sears Tower in Chicago
    c. World Trade Center in New York City
    d. Bank of America Building in San Francisco

64. Which state is Cumberland Lake in?
    a. Kentucky
    b. Virginia
    c. Tennessee
    d. North Carolina

65. What English dessert uses stale cake as its base?
    a. Yorkshire pudding
    b. Cobbler
    c. Trifle
    d. Strawberry slump

66. When someone owns preferred stock in a company, they enjoy what prerogative?
    a. First call on subordinated debentures
    b. First claim on the company's earnings
    c. Guaranteed attendance at stockholder's meetings
    d. Discounts on the company's products

67. What did the Lady Bird Johnson bill abolish?
    a. Charter flights
    b. Nude beaches
    c. Billboards
    d. Bird refuges

68. What French delicacy is classically served with a combination of butter, garlic and parsley?
    a. Frog's legs
    b. Scampi
    c. Shoulder of lamb
    d. Snails

69. What product is most ordered by mail?
    a. Athletic equipment
    b. Clothing
    c. Jewelry
    d. Cosmetics

70. The region known as Patagonia is located in what country?
    a. Albania
    b. Romania
    c. Argentina
    d. Spain

71. What American feast is traditionally cooked over hot rocks?
    a. Clambake
    b. Boston Sunday dinner
    c. Pepper pot
    d. Shrove Tuesday pancakes

72. While used to describe American currency, the word "buck" originates from what?
    a. Horses
    b. Early measurements
    c. Antlers
    d. Deerskins

73. Name the capital of Australia.
    a. Sydney
    b. Canberra
    c. Melbourne
    d. Perth

74. What bread product takes its name from a small Eastern European town?
    a. Bagel
    b. Brioche
    c. Pretzel
    d. Bialy

75. What's the world's largest bank?
    a. Bank of England
    b. Chase Manhattan
    c. Bank of America
    d. Bank of New York

76. Where is the prime meridian located?
    a. Greenland
    b. Iceland
    c. Newfoundland
    d. England

77. What potato dish comes from the Yiddish word for pancake?
    a. Matzo
    b. Kreplach
    c. Latke
    d. Knish

78. Which form of transportation carries the most people from city to city in?
    a. Airplanes
    b. Buses
    c. Trains
    d. Boats

79. Occurring in the Far East, what is a "tsunami?"
    a. Seismic tidal wave
    b. Tornado
    c. Typhoon
    d. Cloud formation

80. What Asian-sounding dish was actually invented in America?
    a. Sushi
    b. Chop Suey
    c. Egg Foo Yong
    d. Teriyaki

81. What city has the world's largest airport in terms of numbers of passengers?
    a. Amsterdam
    b. Atlanta
    c. Chicago
    d. London

82. What's the capital of Switzerland?
    a. Zurich
    b. Basel
    c. Bern
    d. Geneva

83. Name the well-known Japanese one-pot stew.
    a. Teriyaki
    b. Yosenable
    c. Shabu Shabu
    d. Sukiyaki

84. After the U.S., which spends the most advertising dollars per person, what country ties with Switzerland as the next biggest spender?
    a. France
    b. Bermuda
    c. Italy
    d. Japan

85. What country is the city of Timbuktu in?
    a. Mali
    b. Sudan
    c. Tanzania
    d. Uganda

86. At a sushi bar, what is the name for the raw fish served without the rice?
    a. Tekka Maki
    b. Chirashi
    c. Sashimi
    d. Futomaki

87. What department store has the largest sales volume?
    a. Marshall Field
    b. Macy's
    c. Saks Fifth Avenue
    d. Bloomingdale's

88. Name the island located closest to Trinidad.
    a. Jamaica
    b. Cuba
    c. Tobago
    d. Barbados

89. What well-known washing-machine manufacturer also makes cheese?
    a. Westinghouse
    b. General Electric
    c. Kenmore
    d. Maytag

90. On a Monopoly board, Baltic Ave. is tied with what other property as the least expensive?
    a. Illinois Ave.
    b. Reading Railroad
    c. Mediterranean Ave.
    d. Boardwalk

91. Where is the island of Bonaire located?
    a. Off the coast of Venezuela
    b. In the Mediterranean
    c. Near the Mississippi delta
    d. Off the coast of southern France

92. Name the Chinese dish that originally was only served to the emperors.
    a. Moo Goo Gai Pan
    b. Peking duck
    c. Shark fin soup
    d. Bok Choy

93. What do the initials "BMW" stand for?
    a. Best Motor Works
    b. Blackforest Mining Works
    c. Bavarian Motor Works
    d. Berlin Mainz Wien

94. In what state is the Professional Football Hall of Fame?
    a. New York
    b. Ohio
    c. Indiana
    d. Illinois

95. What once-popular spirit is now produced in relatively smaller quantities in the U.S.?
    a. Tennessee whiskey
    b. Bourbon
    c. Rum
    d. Rye whiskey

96. Which of the following beverages do Americans drink the most?
    a. Burgundy
    b. Beer
    c. Chablis
    d. Rosé wine

97. What is a Tuareg?
    a. Currency of Mali
    b. Belgian truffle
    c. An African animal
    d. Nomad of North Africa

98. What country first produced brandy for widescale commercial sale?
    a. France
    b. Spain
    c. Italy
    d. Belgium

99. What country is completely surrounded by the Republic of South Africa?
    a. Swaziland
    b. Lesotho
    c. Namibia
    d. Botswana

100. In which state would you find the oldest synagogue in the United States?
    a. New York
    b. Massachusetts
    c. Rhode Island
    d. Virginia

Answers

1. **B** Mecca. The city was the birthplace of Muhammad.

2. **D** Couscous. It's a pre-cooked semolina made from wheat grain and served as an accompaniment to meat and vegetables.

3. **C** Four. As of April 30, he's finally working for himself and not for the government.

4. **B** England. It's a chain of hills which run from the Scottish border to Derbyshire in central England.

5. **A** Dim Sum. These Cantonese appetizers literally mean "to dot the heart." They include steamed and fried dumplings, spring rolls, and noodle packages of meat and vegetables.

6. **D** William Post. He introduced Grape Nuts in 1897, which was followed by Post Toasties in 1922.

7. **B** Salzburg. This city derives its name from the salt mines in the area.

8. **C** Corn. The whiskey has a slightly sweet taste from the corn. It was named after Bourbon County, Kentucky, and must contain 51% corn.

9. **C** Frank Woolworth. His first store was located in Utica, New York.

10. **D** Nevada. The state also has the nation's highest suicide rate.

11. **A** Thousand-year-old eggs. Not as old as they sound, they are duck eggs that are covered with a mixture of lime, pine ash, salt and rice husks for two to four months before eating.

12. **C** Burma Shave. Among its most popular copy was: "Every shave/now can snore/six more minutes/than before."

13. **D** Arizona. Privately purchased in 1968 for $4.5 million, the bridge was shipped block by block to its present site and reassembled.

14. **C** VSOP. Standing for "Very Superior Old Pale," it meant that the cognac was natural and not flavored or darkened with additives.

15. **C** Bulova watches. The company paid nine dollars for the first commercial minute of television advertising in July 1941.

16. **B** Leningrad. Many of the great works of art there were brought to Russia by Catherine the Great.

17. **D** Pinot noir. It's used to make Burgundy with its skin, and without its skin it's used to make champagne.

18. **B** Frederick Porsche. According to legend, this German designer fashioned the automobile at Hitler's request.

19. **A** Georgia. It's located in the churchyard of Atlanta's Ebenezer Baptist Church where King and his father preached.

20. **C** Leek. It was originally worn in the caps of the Welsh to distinguish them in battle.

21. **C** Rezin Bowie. He was Jim Bowie's brother and was evidently overshadowed by Jim.

22. **B** Utah. The park was named after its first settler, Ebenezer Bryce, who said of it, "It's a helluva place to lose a cow!"

23. **A** Italy. The country not only produces the most wine in the world, but it also has the highest per capita consumption, amounting to 130 bottles per year.

24. **C** Coors beer. The film turned out to be one of Reynolds' most popular and profitable features.

25. **D** Egypt. It is a part of the ruins of ancient Thebes found at Luxor.

26. **B** Almonds. They're crushed and mixed with sugar and egg whites before being shaped and colored.

27. **C**   Polaroid camera. He invented it after his daughter asked to see her picture immediately after it was taken.

28. **D**   Belize. This former British colony is one of the major unexplored centers of the ancient Mayan civilization.

29. **A**   Gelatin. It's dried and powdered for use in desserts, aspics and pie fillings. It's also alleged to be good for fingernail strength and growth.

30. **C**   The New York Stock Exchange was formed there. Founded in 1790, The New York Stock Exchange is the nation's largest, handling more than 70 percent (in market value) of all stock transactions in the U.S.

31. **D**   Turkey. For ten years the city of Troy was besieged by Mycenaean Greeks.

32. **C**   Ruth Wakefield. Owner of the Toll House restaurant in Whitman, Massachusetts, she substituted a cut-up chocolate bar for nuts in a batch of cookies. It was 1930 and the cookies became known as "Toll House Cookies."

33. **D**   Queen Elizabeth I. Her reign produced such literary figures as Spenser, Bacon, and Shakespeare.

34. **B**   Pakistan. The kingdom is known for the healthiest and happiest people in the world.

35. **D**   Chocolate. In 18th century Central America, only those over the age of sixty were permitted to drink chocolate; any others were threatened with excommunication for imbibing.

36. **A**   Sears. The chain was founded in 1893 by Richard Sears and Alvah Roebuck to sell watches.

37. **B**   The Seychelles. This island group in the Indian Ocean contains 85 islands.

38. **D**   The Arabs. They were drinking coffee in 850 A.D., and it was exported from a town in southwestern Arabia named Mocha. It didn't appear in Europe until 1517.

39. **B**   Pennsylvania. Released prior to the accident, the film "China Syndrome" had a line noting that a nuclear accident could destroy a state the size of Pennsylvania.

40. **C**   Ghana. The country became a member of the British Commonwealth in 1957.

41. **B**   Garlic. In China it was used to ward off the evil eye, while in India it was found to improve the voice, intellect, and complexion. The ancient Romans fed it to their soldiers to give them courage.

42. **A**   Cough and cold remedies. The second most frequent purchase is aspirin.

43. **C**   Cave exploration. If you enjoy this pastime, you can join the National Speleological Society in Louisville, Kentucky.

44. **A**   Noodles. They appear in almost every culture. Marco Polo did not bring them back to Italy, as Italian rules governing the shape and size of noodles predated his trip by 70 years.

45. **C**   Texas. It's a $2.5 billion dollar industry in that state. Iowa is next with $1.8 billion.

46. **B**   Micronesia. These islands include the sites of some of the bloodiest fighting of World War II, particularly on Guam and Saipan.

47. **C**   Pierre Franey. He's currently a food columnist for the *New York Times* and a collaborator with Craig Claiborne on many cookbooks.

48. **D**   Can of condensed milk. He not only invented the process of evaporating milk, but he also patented processes for concentrating fruit juices and other beverages.

49. **A**   Peru. It's the highest navigable body of water in the world.

50. **C**   Henri Soulé. Under his tutelage at his world famous Le Pavillon restaurant in New York, legions of chefs went on to open their own restaurants.

51. **B**   Headache remedy. The inventor of Coca-Cola sold his formula for a whopping $1,750.

52. **C**   Kauai. It is also known as the "Garden Isle."

53. **D**   Welsh rabbit. Consisting of melted cheddar cheese and beer, it's mistakenly called "rarebit" since it was devised by a Welsh housewife who was forced to cook cheese when her husband came home empty-handed from the hunt.

54. **B**   Ruth Cleveland. She was the daughter of President Grover Cleveland.

55. **C**   Kampala. The city has a population of over 300,000.

56. **B**   Julia Child. Learning to cook at the Cordon Bleu while her husband was stationed in France, she went on to write *Mastering the*

Art of French Cooking, which led to her popular television show.

57. **A** Tennis shoe. Fully half of all shoes sold in the U.S. are tennis shoes.

58. **D** Washington. The islands lie between Washington and Canada's Vancouver Island.

59. **C** Fettucine. Both restaurants are named Alfredo and both regard the dish, served with butter, cream and cheese, to be their claim to fame.

60. **C** Harvard. The university presently has a net worth of $1.45 billion.

61. **A** Germany. It's located in the Black Forest and became a rendezvous for pleasure in the 19th century.

62. **C** U.S. Senate. Senate Bean Soup was named after the upper house. It's supposed to invigorate worn-out Senators.

63. **B** Sears Tower in Chicago. The skyscraper is measured at 1,454 feet. The tallest structure in the U.S. is the TV Tower at Blanchard, North Dakota, which measures 2,063 feet.

64. **A** Kentucky. It was formed by a dam on the Cumberland river which transformed mountaintops into islands.

65. **C** Trifle. This venerable dessert is a combination of liquor-soaked cake, custard, whipped cream and jam.

66. **B** First claim on the company's earnings. Stock regulations are set by the governing board of each stock exchange and by the Securities and Exchange Commission.

67. **C** Billboards. At the urging of President Johnson's wife, all billboards on primary highways that were not zoned commercial or industrial were to be razed by July 1, 1970.

68. **D** Snails. Called "escargots" in French, the choicest snails are bred in Burgundy and feed on the leaves of vintage vines.

69. **B** Clothing. It approximates $2 billion a year. The second product most ordered by mail is insurance.

70. **C** Argentina. The region is found in the south of the country with frigid temperatures at the southernmost tip.

71. **A** Clambake. Clams, lobsters, corn and potatoes are covered with seaweed and steamed from the heat of the hot rocks underneath.

72. **D** Deerskins. One of the very first forms of currency in the U.S. was the deerskin.

73. **B** Canberra. The rivalry between Melbourne and Sydney made it necessary to establish the capital elsewhere.

74. **D** Bialy. The round roll topped with onions and sometimes poppy or sesame seeds originated in the town of Bialystok.

75. **C** Bank of America. It presently has assets nearing $85 billion.

76. **D** England. It runs through the original site of the Royal Observatory at Greenwich outside London.

77. **C** Latke. These are potato pancakes made with grated onions and eggs and traditionally served at Chanukah with applesauce.

78. **B** Buses. Over 378 million passengers a year use buses which are followed by airplanes which carry 308 million passengers.

79. **A** Seismic tidal wave. The highest ever recorded was 220 feet tall.

80. **B** Chop Suey. The first wave of Chinese immigrants from Canton invented the dish in the late 19th century.

81. **C** Chicago. O'Hare Airport handles approximately 44 million passengers a year.

82. **C** Bern. It's one of Europe's best kept cities with arcaded streets and decorative fountains.

83. **D** Sukiyaki. Derived from the words, "suki" which means "hoe" and "yaki" meaning "to broil," the dish originated in feudal times, when peasants would steam meat and cook hoes it on their hoes over the fire.

84. **B** Bermuda. Along with Switzerland, this country spends $110 per person per year in advertising.

85. **A** Mali. This walled Islamic city was once barred to infidels and is now accessible.

86. **C** Sashimi. It's normally served amidst beautifully sculpted vegetables.

87. **B** Macy's. It does a volume of over $650 million per year.

88. **C** Tobago. It is the most southerly of the West Indies Caribbean islands.

89. **D**   Maytag. They own the Maytag Dairy Farms in Iowa and were recently selected to produce the new "fancy" blue cheese developed at Iowa State University because of their award-winning herd of holstein-friesian cattle.

90. **C**   Mediterranean Ave. These properties can be bought for a mere $60.

91. **A**   Off the coast of Venezuela. As part of the Netherlands Antilles, the native residents speak a dialect called "Papumento" which is a combination of Dutch, Spanish and Creole words.

92. **B**   Peking duck. After days of preparation, the duck's skin is served with pancakes, scallions and hoisin sauce while the meat is served separately.

93. **C**   Bavarian Motor Works. Rarely seen in the U.S. until recently, the BMW is now one of the best-selling luxury foreign cars.

94. **B**   Ohio. It's located in Canton, Ohio, where the NFL was founded in 1929.

95. **D**   Rye whiskey. The term "rye" is often mistakenly used as a generic name for blended whiskeys.

96. **B**   Beer. Americans drink eleven times more beer than wine.

97. **D**   Nomad of North Africa. Occupying the western and central Sahara along the Niger, these tall, nomadic people speak Hamitic.

98. **A**   France. While brandy is produced throughout the country, the two most notable regions are Cognac and Armagnac.

99. **B**   Lesotho. It was founded by a union of Basotho tribes as a land where blacks could live in freedom and became independent in 1966.

100. **C**   Rhode Island. In Newport you'll find the Touro Synagogue which was built in 1763.

TWO

Science

(Animals, Plants, Medicine, Health, Space, Science, Technology)

1. What kind of clouds usually precede rainstorms?
   a. Cumulonimbus
   b. Cirrus
   c. Altostratus
   d. Altocumulus

2. What is the smallest flightless bird?
   a. Penguin
   b. Kiwi
   c. Cassowary
   d. Emu

3. Who gave the first complete description of spermatozoa?
   a. Niklaas Hartsoeker
   b. Galen
   c. Gabriello Fallopio
   d. Antony van Leeuwenhoek

4. What is the fastest running animal?
   a. Cheetah
   b. Panther
   c. Ostrich
   d. Cougar

5. Who invented the rocking chair?
   a. Isaac Newton
   b. Thomas Jefferson
   c. Benjamin Franklin
   d. Eli Whitney

6. What is Cheyne-Stokes respiration?
   a. Breathing with mouth open
   b. Irregular breathing
   c. Holding one's breath
   d. Vomit in the lungs

7. What common American fruit is distinguished into types according to the ease with which its seed separates from its flesh?
   a. Peach
   b. Avocado
   c. Plum
   d. Apricot

8. Who was the commander of Apollo 8?
   a. Wally Schirra
   b. Scott Carpenter
   c. Neil Armstrong
   d. Frank Borman

9. What virus causes cold sores?
   a. Herpes genitalis
   b. Herpes zoster
   c. Herpes simplex
   d. Candida albicans

10. What animal, which feeds on blood, can consume up to ten times its body weight in one meal?
    a. Vampire bat
    b. Leech
    c. Rat
    d. Cobra

11. What famous scientist was offered the presidency of Israel?
    a. Max Planck
    b. Chaim Weizmann
    c. Albert Einstein
    d. Albert Abraham Michelson

12. For what function is vitamin K essential?
    a. Red blood cell production
    b. Blood clotting
    c. Calcium absorption
    d. Oxygenation

13. What sea animal is famous for having given its body as the symbol for a major international company?
    a. Cockle
    b. Oyster
    c. Jackknife clam
    d. Scallop

14. What is the name of the first lunar module to orbit the moon?
    a. "Spider"
    b. "Columbus"
    c. "Snoopy"
    d. "Discovery"

15. Who can have hemophilia?
    a. Only females
    b. Only males
    c. Males and Y-chromosome females
    d. Only females with blood type O

16. What is the only fish with a prehensile tale—one with which it can grasp?
    a. Eel
    b. Squid
    c. Sea horse
    d. Thresher shark

17. What planet has the most satellites in its orbit?
    a. Jupiter
    b. Saturn
    c. Uranus
    d. Neptune

18. What gives blood its red color?
    a. Gamma globulin
    b. Platelets
    c. Hemoglobin
    d. Plasma

19. What is the largest reptile?
    a. Alligator
    b. Giant tortoise
    c. Sea serpent
    d. Crocodile

20. Of the seven original Mercury astronauts, who was the youngest?
    a. Gus Grissom
    b. Alan Shepard
    c. Gordon Cooper
    d. John Glenn

21. What recreational activity burns up the most calories per hour?
    a. Jogging
    b. Swimming
    c. Racquetball
    d. Football

22. While the jackass is commonly thought to be a donkey, what species of bird also has a jackass in its family?
    a. Bluebird
    b. Sea gull
    c. Penguin
    d. Crow

23. Joseph Priestley is famous in the field of chemistry for his discovery of what element?
    a. Radium
    b. Uranium
    c. Oxygen
    d. Mercury

24. Why is the left lung smaller than the right lung?
    a. The left lung is more prone to infection
    b. The left lung evolved gradually from mammals having only one lung
    c. More people have better developed right sides
    d. To make room for the heart

25. Thought of as a fruit native to Hawaii, where was the pineapple actually first found by Europeans?
    a. Malaysia
    b. Tahiti
    c. Australia
    d. Brazil

26. Who is the youngest Nobel Prize winner?
    a. Albert Einstein
    b. Francis Peyton Rous
    c. William Lawrence Bragg
    d. Thomas Edison

27. What is a keloid?
    a. A chemotherapy drug
    b. A scar that keeps growing
    c. The type of fat cell that makes up cellulite
    d. An amoeba that causes dysentery

28. What toxic plant was used by the ancient Greeks to put criminals to death?
    a. Almond shells
    b. Apricot pits
    c. Hemlock tree leaves
    d. Hemlock

29. Who invented the phrase "three, two, one, lift-off"?
    a. Fritz Lang
    b. Robert H. Goddard
    c. Chris Craft
    d. Wernher von Braun

30. What is psoriasis?
    a. Thickened, scaly patches of skin
    b. Patches of raw skin
    c. Severely dehydrated skin
    d. The most common form of eczema

31. What sea animal is used in the home, but not as food?
    a. Loofah
    b. Algae
    c. Snail
    d. Sponge

32. What was the great healing discovery made by Sir Alexander Fleming?
    a. Tetracycline
    b. Sulfa
    c. Aspirin
    d. Penicillin

33. What was the life expectancy of prehistoric man?
    a. 18 years
    b. 60 years
    c. 35 years
    d. 75 years

34. What relative of the starfish can lose its entire digestive system and then regenerate it completely?
    a. Sea horse
    b. Sea cucumber
    c. Anemone
    d. Hydra

35. Who invented the television set?
    a. Henry J. Kaiser
    b. J. Robert Oppenheimer
    c. Philo Taylor Farnsworth
    d. Joseph Henry

36. On what area of the body was the earliest known surgery performed?
    a. Teeth
    b. Feet
    c. Skull
    d. Stomach

37. What animal is known for emitting squeaks and using echoes to help it avoid running into obstacles?
    a. Mouse
    b. Bat
    c. Rabbit
    d. Whale

38. What was Alan Shepard's last mission?
    a. Apollo/Soyuz
    b. Skylab
    c. Apollo 14
    d. Apollo 11

39. Who spread the first major epidemic of syphilis?
    a. The Huns
    b. Marco Polo's soldiers
    c. Casanova
    d. Columbus's sailors

40. What is the purpose of the moth's antennae?
    a. Hearing
    b. Communication
    c. Smell
    d. Avoidance of danger

41. What is the temperature on the surface of the sun?
    a. 10,300 degrees F.
    b. 100,000 degrees F.
    c. 500,000 degrees F.
    d. 1,000,000 degrees F.

42. Who was the father of medical classification?
    a. Bernardino Ramazzini
    b. Linnaeus
    c. Boissier de Sauvages
    d. Hippocrates

43. What tree is struck by lightning more frequently than any other?
    a. Elm
    b. Oak
    c. Chestnut
    d. Weeping willow

44. Who was the first man to build a liquid-fueled rocket and fire it?
    a. Wernher von Braun
    b. Herman Oberth
    c. Robert H. Goddard
    d. Robert Esnault-Pelterie

45. What does "cytotoxic" mean?
    a. Killing by radiation
    b. Cell-poisoning
    c. Allergic reaction
    d. Cancer-causing

46. What jet-black wood is known for its use in cabinetry and in the construction of musical instruments, notably the piano and clarinet?
    a. Teak
    b. Mahogany
    c. Rosewood
    d. Ebony

47. What was Thomas Edison's first patented invention?
    a. Light bulb
    b. Telegraph
    c. Voting machine
    d. Phonograph

48. What medicinal herb has been valued like a jewel in China and still commands a high price in the West today?
    a. Oolong
    b. Ginseng
    c. Mandrake
    d. Ma-huang

49. While the palm branch is a symbol of victory, what plant has been associated with peace?
    a. Rose
    b. Olive
    c. Cherry
    d. Tobacco

50. What is the region of charged radioactive particles above the earth's atmosphere?
    a. Northern lights
    b. Solar winds
    c. Aurora borealis
    d. Van Allen belt

51. Who was the Greek god of healing?
    a. Chiron
    b. Asclepius
    c. Apollo
    d. Athena

52. What is the Japanese garden art of growing dwarfed trees called?
    a. Origami
    b. Ramaki
    c. Ajuga
    d. Bonsai

53. What is the widely used substance developed by Du Pont chemist Roy Plunkett?
    a. Nylon
    b. Teflon
    c. Plexiglas
    d. Plastic

54. During the Middle Ages, physicians and apothecaries belonged to the same guild as what other group?
    a. Barbers
    b. Butchers
    c. Artists
    d. Surgeons

55. What annual plant is the most important fiber-producing crop in the world?
    a. Soybean
    b. Cotton
    c. Silk
    d. Hemp

56. What would be the apparent color of a pure red card when seen in a pure green light?
    a. Greenish-red
    b. No color
    c. Mauve
    d. Brown

57. In Greek mythology, what were the winged monsters that befouled food called?
    a. Circes
    b. Scyllas
    c. Harpies
    d. Charybdis

58. In times of famine, how did the early Eskimos treat the elderly?
    a. They were the last to be given food
    b. They clubbed them to death
    c. They ate them
    d. They were abandoned unsheltered in the snow

59. What is the name of the device that casts the shadow on a sundial?
    a. Dialectic
    b. Gnomon
    c. Elbo
    d. Sunapee

60. From what plant do morphine and codeine come?
    a. Heliotrope
    b. Curare
    c. Poppy
    d. Belladonna

61. Why does your voice sound one way when you hear a recording of it, and another way when you hear yourself speak?
    a. Voice goes through the eustachian tube, bypassing the eardrum
    b. Voice is transmitted through the bones of the skull
    c. We're more sensitive to the distortions of recordings
    d. Voice echoes slightly in the sinus cavities in your head

62. Why is the sky blue?
    a. Reflects the sea
    b. Air is naturally blue
    c. Heavy oxygen content
    d. Light spectrum is scattered

63. What plant did painter Claude Monet immortalize in many of his most beautiful impressionist paintings?
    a. Carnations
    b. Lilies
    c. Orchids
    d. Water lilies

64. What is the drug that reduces the risk of organ transplant rejection?
    a. Beta blockers
    b. Cyclosporin
    c. Monoclonal antibodies
    d. Corticosteroids

65. What is the common name for caisson disease?
    a. Dry heaves
    b. Motion sickness
    c. The bends
    d. Rupture

66. In what way is the manufacture of rayon different from that of nylon or Orlon?
    a. Made in the dark

b. Made from organic materials
c. Spun instead of woven
d. Made in cold temperatures

67. What fungal substance has long been consumed by Mexican Indians for its hallucinogenic properties?
   a. Peyote
   b. Opium poppy
   c. Psilocybin
   d. Lotus

68. Who introduced the term "anesthesia"?
   a. Oliver Wendell Holmes
   b. Joseph Priestley
   c. Horace Wells
   d. John C. Warren

69. Albert Einstein's theory of relativity flew in the face of whose laws of mechanics?
   a. Ptolemy
   b. Archimedes
   c. Isaac Newton
   d. Ernest Rutherford

70. What is the Malay climbing palm whose parts are used for fine woven baskets and wicker work?
   a. Bamboo
   b. Hemp
   c. Amok
   d. Rattan

71. What causes acne?
   a. Eating greasy foods
   b. Dirt and bacteria on the skin
   c. Overactive sebaceous glands
   d. Imbalance of the hormone estrogen

72. On the Richter scale, a 6.0 tremor is how many times more powerful than one that measures 5.0?
   a. Two
   b. Ten
   c. Six
   d. Four

73. What cereal crop is the principal food for over 60 percent of mankind?
   a. Potatoes
   b. Corn
   c. Wheat
   d. Rice

74. What is a greenstick fracture?
   a. An impacted fracture
   b. An incomplete break in the bone
   c. A broken bone sticking out of the skin
   d. A comminuted fracture

75. Quartz, feldspar and mica are common in what type of rock?
   a. Igneous
   b. Shale
   c. Porphyry
   d. Limestone

76. The male of what species of insect can continue to copulate and complete the fertilization of the female even after she has decapitated him in the midst of the act?
   a. Black widow
   b. Snout beetle
   c. Praying mantis
   d. Tarantula

77. What is cyanosis?
   a. Carbon monoxide poisoning
   b. Bluish coloring of the skin
   c. Cyanide poisoning
   d. More blood in the veins than in the arteries

78. What is studied in a cloud chamber?
   a. Types of clouds
   b. Lightning
   c. High-energy subatomic particles
   d. Tornadoes

79. What bird is best known for laying its eggs in the nests of other birds?
   a. Nightingale
   b. Mockingbird
   c. Blue jay
   d. Cuckoo

80. What is tachycardia?
   a. Cardiac arrest
   b. Irregular breathing
   c. Abnormally fast heart rate
   d. Hyperventilation

81. What were X-rays originally called?
   a. Alpha rays
   b. Roentgen rays
   c. Y-rays
   d. Kappa rays

82. What is the largest member of the bear family?
   a. Kodiak bear
   b. Polar bear
   c. Grizzly bear
   d. Asian black bear

83. What does a sphygmomanometer measure?
   a. Lung capacity
   b. Body temperature
   c. Heart rate
   d. Blood pressure

84. How did Galileo get into trouble with the Inquisition?
    a. Invented the telescope
    b. Reinforced Copernicus's theory
    c. Found the moons of Jupiter
    d. Built the Tower of Pisa

85. What mammal, which once numbered 60 million, was reduced to a population of around 550 by the 1880s?
    a. Moose
    b. Caribou
    c. Buffalo
    d. Brown bear

86. What is the leading cause of death in the United States?
    a. Cancer
    b. Accidents
    c. Cardiovascular disease
    d. Diabetes

87. What is the brightest star in the sky?
    a. Ursa Major
    b. Sirius
    c. Venus
    d. Arcturus

88. What is the most well-known example of the order of mammals known as monotremes?
    a. Kangaroo
    b. Platypus
    c. Aardvark
    d. Porcupine

89. What is an oncogene?
    a. Tumor gene
    b. Cloned amino acid
    c. Sex-determining gene
    d. Hair color gene

90. What was the code name of the atomic bomb that was dropped on Nagasaki?
    a. Red Dragon
    b. Samson
    c. Hercules
    d. Fat Man

91. What is the most inclusive distinguishing characteristic of the order of mammals known as marsupials?
    a. Pouch
    b. Upright position
    c. Absence of an internal placenta
    d. No nipples to nurse young

92. What causes cretinism?
    a. Brain damage
    b. Thyroid deficiency
    c. Malnutrition
    d. Inadequate oxygen to the brain

93. How did the man who endowed the Nobel Peace Prize make all his money?
    a. Plastics
    b. Railroads
    c. Explosives
    d. Cloth

94. What is the more precise terminology for evergreen trees?
    a. Deciduous
    b. Pine
    c. Fir
    d. Conifer

95. How should a frostbitten hand be treated?
    a. Soak in the hottest water tolerable
    b. Soak in lukewarm water
    c. Rub briskly until circulation comes back
    d. Soak in 40 degree F. water

96. What was the name of the command module of the Apollo 11 mission?
    a. "Enterprise"
    b. "America"
    c. "Liberty"
    d. "Columbia"

97. What plant has been valued for over 3500 years as a dye, perfume, medicine, and spice?
    a. Goldenrod
    b. Indigo
    c. Saffron
    d. Persimmon

98. What is a myocardial infarction?
    a. Heart attack
    b. Congestive heart failure
    c. Cardiomyopathy
    d. Heart valve flutter

99. What was the name of the Mercury 7 capsule flown by Alan Shepard?
    a. "Friendship 7"
    b. "Liberty 7"
    c. "Freedom 7"
    d. "Rover 7"

100. Where is a baby's pulse taken?
    a. From the femoral artery of the thigh
    b. From the carotid artery of the neck
    c. At the wrist
    d. At the heart

Answers

1. **A** Cumulonimbus. These clouds often tower 20,000 feet.

2. **B** Kiwi. It grows to the size of a chicken, while a bird like the penguin—which many consider to be small—can grow to four feet and weigh 75 pounds.

3. **D** Antony van Leeuwenhoek. He made his discovery in 1677 using a microscope that he designed.

4. **A** Cheetah. This animal can achieve speeds in excess of 60 miles per hour.

5. **C** Benjamin Franklin. He also started the first fire company in Philadelphia.

6. **B** Irregular breathing. It often occurs with heart failure. In terminally ill patients it may indicate that death will occur soon.

7. **A** Peach. Peaches are called either clingstone or freestone.

8. **D** Frank Borman. Launched on December 21, 1968, this Apollo mission was the first manned flight around the moon.

9. **C** Herpes simplex. It is commonly thought to be spread by kissing.

10. **B** Leech. When feeding on its host—sometimes a human—the animal secretes an anticoagulant into the blood so it can feed freely.

11. **C** Albert Einstein. He refused, saying that he had no head for human problems.

12. **B** Blood clotting. Vitamin K is found in leafy green vegetables.

13. **D** Scallop. The symbol for Shell Oil Company. The scallop can escape its enemies by snapping its shell halves together.

14. **C** "Snoopy." Launched May 18, 1969, the lunar module descended to within nine miles of the lunar surface.

15. **B** Only males. But the disease is carried by females. Hemophilia is a deficiency in blood-clotting ability.

16. **C** Sea horse. It uses its tail to cling to seaweed, and also has the distinction of being a species in which the male looks after the eggs which hatch out of a pouch in his belly.

17. **B** Saturn. It has 17 confirmed satellites plus 5 more that have been sited but unconfirmed.

18. **C** Hemoglobin. This is the protein of red blood cells which carries oxygen.

19. **D** Crocodile. Some crocodiles are so large and fierce that they can feed on animals up to the size of a cow.

20. **C** Gordon Cooper. He was 32 at the time of the selection on April 9, 1959. John Glenn was the oldest at 37.

21. **B** Swimming. The average person consumes 720 calories per hour while swimming, but only 480 calories per hour while jogging.

22. **C** Penguin. One of the 18 species of this bird is called the jackass penguin.

23. **C** Oxygen. He also came up with the name "rubber" for the soft, bouncy product.

24. **D** To make room for the heart. Covered by a thin membrane called the pleura, which allows them to move freely during breathing, the lungs expand and contract by the combined movement of the diaphragm and the rib cage.

25. **D** Brazil. Pineapple was exported to several other countries after 1500 before coming to Hawaii around 1800.

26. **C** William Lawrence Bragg. At the age of 25, he shared the award for physics in 1915.

27. **B** A scar that keeps growing. Keloids are usually harmless.

28. **D** Hemlock. This is an herb and not the hemlock tree we know. The poisonous substance is used as a narcotic pain reliever.

29. **A** Fritz Lang. It came from his 1929 film *Die Frau im Mond (The Woman in the Moon)*.

30. **A** Thickened, scaly patches of skin. Psoriasis happens when cells are produced faster than they are worn off.

31. **D** Sponge. It is among the lowest animals except for protozoa.

32. **D** Penicillin. It was discovered quite by accident in 1928.

33. **C** 35 years. This is determined from the bones of Paleolithic, Mesolithic and Neolithic periods. Men apparently lived longer than women, who may have had less to eat and frequently died in childbirth.

34. **B** Sea cucumber. While this is a rather extraordinary feat of regeneration, many lizards and starfish can also regenerate parts of their bodies.

35. **C** Philo Taylor Farnsworth. He did this in the late 1920s.

36. **C** Skull. Skulls discovered in French caves, which date from 10,000 to 700 B.C. have portions cut out, but it's unknown whether the operations were performed for religious or medical purposes.

37. **B** Bat. While only certain species of bats have this radar, certain aquatic animals, like whales, use it to locate food or to communicate.

38. **C** "Apollo 14". Launched on January 31, 1971, the craft made a moon landing on February 5, 1971.

39. **D** Columbus's sailors. They brought it back with them from the New World.

40. **C** Smell. The male's antennae are finely feathered to pick up even minute scents, such as that of the female ready to mate.

41. **A** 10,300 degrees F. The temperature at the sun's core is estimated to be 35,000,000 degrees F.

42. **C** Boissier de Sauvages. While Linnaeus popularized classification with his work in botany and zoology, his medical classifications were useless.

43. **B** Oak. The odd connection between oaks and lightning has made them particularly fertile trees in terms of mythology and lore.

44. **C** Robert H. Goddard. He accomplished this on March 16, 1926. He also designed the first practical automatic steering device for rockets.

45. **B** Cell-poisoning. Cytotoxic drugs are used in cancer treatment and sometimes in suppressing the immune system.

46. **D** Ebony. It's used for the black keys on pianos and the cabinets of many fine grand pianos.

47. **C** Voting machine. Edison designed it in the 1860s.

48. **B** Ginseng. Although there's no scientific data or proof, it's believed to help impotence, high blood pressure, diabetes and tuberculosis.

49. **B** Olive. It has become so emblematic of peace that a peace offering can be referred to as an "olive branch."

50. **D** Van Allen belt. It was named for James Van Allen, an American astrophysicist, in 1958.

51. **B** Asclepius. The large temples dedicated to this god were the centers of healing for centuries.

52. **D** Bonsai. This art is so refined that only certain containers can be used that will accentuate the design of the tree.

53. **B** Teflon. Plunkett discovered this substance while working on refrigerants.

54. **C** Artists. They were grouped with them because of their common use of powders. Surgeons had a separate guild which included barbers.

55. **B** Cotton. The crop is grown in nearly 70 countries and is widespread in the U.S. and the U.S.S.R.

56. **B** No color. The card reflects only the red portion of the spectrum, which is nonexistent in the green.

57. **C** Harpies. They were said to have had faces of old hags, ears of a bear and bodies of a bird.

58. **D** They were abandoned unsheltered in the snow. Almost all Eskimo property is communal, and the Inuit (as they prefer to be called) have a religion that's rich in mythology.

59. **B** Gnomon. It comes from the Greek word meaning "one who knows."

60. **C** Poppy. Morphine was isolated from the opium poppy in 1803. Known as alkaloids, morphine and codeine are powerful anesthetics and tranquilizers, and, in excess, can cause hallucinations.

61. **B** Voice is transmitted through the bones of skull. Because the voice doesn't travel the normal path through the bones of the middle ear, we hear ourselves differently.

62. **D** Light spectrum is scattered. The shorter (blue) end of the visible light spectrum is scattered the most by the atmosphere which gives the sky a predominantly blue hue.

63. **D** Water lilies. Growing in the northern and southern hemispheres and in the tropics, they exhibit a wide range of colors.

64. **B** Cyclosporin. It has the unfortunate side effect of knocking out the body's immune system, which leaves the patient susceptible to infection.

65. **C** The bends. When divers are at considerable depths, where pressure is great, concentration of nitrogen dissolves in their blood. When they return to the surface and air pressure decreases, the gas reappears as embolisms in the bloodstream.

66. **B** Made from organic materials. Rayon is made from cellulose which is found in the woody tissue of all plants.

67. **C** Psilocybin. Often used by some tribes as part of their religious rites, some species of these fungi can be deadly.

68. **A** Oliver Wendell Holmes. Many people forget that Holmes was a physician as well as a literary figure. His son served on the Supreme Court from 1902 until 1932.

69. **C** Isaac Newton. The theory of relativity conflicted with Newton's assumption that one could assure oneself of the simultaneity of occurrence and observation.

70. **D** Rattan. Any rattan that is over 20mm in diameter is called cane.

71. **C** Overactive sebaceous glands. Some form of acne afflicts 90 to 95 percent of the population between the ages of 13 and 23.

72. **B** Ten. The scale was named after the American Charles Richter and is a logarithmic scale.

73. **D** Rice. Ninety percent of the world's rice is grown and eaten in Asia.

74. **B** An incomplete break in the bone. This happens frequently in children because their bones have not yet completely hardened.

75. **A** Igneous. This type of rock results from the cooling and solidification of molten matter from the earth's interior.

76. **C** Praying mantis. The female kills and eats the male at various stages of mating.

77. **B** Bluish coloring of the skin. This is often a sign of severe respiratory problems.

78. **C** High-energy subatomic particles. They leave a momentary track that can be captured on film.

79. **D** Cuckoo. The host bird feeds the baby cuckoo as if it were her own. The height of ingratitude is when the young cuckoo, larger than the other chicks, often pushes the host's young out of the nest.

80. **C** Abnormally fast heart rate. It's often over 100 beats per minute at rest.

81. **B** Roentgen rays. They were named after their discoverer who won the first Nobel Prize for physics in 1901.

82. **A** Kodiak bear. These bears can grow to nine feet in length and often weigh in excess of 1600 pounds.

83. **D** Blood pressure. Pressure is measured at the brachial artery in the arm (for consistency) in millimeters of mercury.

84. **B** Reinforced Copernicus's theory. Initially backing Copernicus's belief that the earth was not the fixed center of the universe, Galileo later recanted his position.

85. **C** Buffalo. These large and once prevalent American land mammals are now protected and have a population of about 25,000.

86. **C** Cardiovascular disease. It kills about one million people per year, which is almost twice as many as all other causes *combined*!

87. **B** Sirius. Known as the Dog Star, it's located near the constellation Orion.

88. **B** Platypus. These animals are the only egg-laying mammals.

89. **A**   Tumor gene. Oncogenes provide the genetic code for the production of proteins that can cause cancerous changes in cells.

90. **D**   Fat Man. The bomb that exploded three days earlier at Hiroshima was called Little Boy.

91. **C**   Absence of internal placenta. Unformed young fetuses must climb from the vagina to a place where nourishment can be found—in the pouch of a kangaroo, for instance.

92. **B**   Thyroid deficiency. If it occurs in childhood or earlier, it will lead to mental retardation and abnormal body development.

93. **C**   Explosives. The Swedish chemist Alfred Nobel made the bulk of his fortune from the invention and marketing of dynamite and munitions.

94. **D**   Conifer. The word refers to the cone-type structures which house the tree's seeds. Trees in this group include pines, cypresses, cedars, firs and spruces.

95. **B**   Soak in lukewarm water. Rubbing a frostbitten area can cause serious damage.

96. **D**   "Columbia." Neil Armstrong was the commander of this historic mission.

97. **C**   Saffron. It's the dried stigmata of a type of crocus. Used to dye the robe of some religious orders, it is also a very expensive spice used in cooking.

98. **A**   Heart attack. The heart muscle dies due to inadequate oxygen supply.

99. **C**   "Freedom 7." Shepard was the fifth person to walk on the moon's surface.

100. **D**   At the heart. It's here that it's felt most easily.

THREE

History

(European History, American History, Religion, Mythology)

1. Martin Luther was ordered to appear before the Imperial Diet in what city?
   a. Wittenberg
   b. Augsburg
   c. Worms
   d. Rome

2. For whom was the Great Pyramid of Giza built?
   a. Akhenaton
   b. Tutankhamen
   c. Cleopatra
   d. Cheops

3. What did Thomas à Kempis write?
   a. Unam Sanctam
   b. The Imitation of Christ
   c. The Book of Common Prayer
   d. The Syllabus of Errors

4. Who was the first king of Israel?
   a. Herod
   b. Solomon
   c. David
   d. Saul

5. Name the religious rebel who was ordered by the Council of Constance to be burned at the stake.
   a. Savonarola
   b. John Constance
   c. Martin Luther
   d. John Huss

6. Under whose leadership was the Parthenon built?
   a. Alexander the Great
   b. Pericles
   c. Ptolemy I
   d. Menelaus

7. The word "cathedral" is derived from the word "cathedra," which has what meaning?
   a. Throne
   b. Shrine
   c. Cross
   d. Tower

8. Who was the first European to discover America?
   a. Amerigo Vespucci
   b. Leif Ericsson
   c. Eric the Red
   d. Christopher Columbus

9. What pope in 1073 ordered the married bishops of Germany to give up their wives?
   a. Leo I
   b. Innocent III
   c. Boniface VIII
   d. Gregory VII

10. What city was ruled by Cosimo and Lorenzo de' Medici?
    a. Milan
    b. Venice
    c. Florence
    d. Rome

11. Where was Jesus' last earthly appearance?
    a. The Church of the Holy Sepulchre
    b. The Garden of Gethsemane
    c. The Mount of Olives
    d. The Temple of Jerusalem

12. Who was Prince Temuchin?
    a. Buddha
    b. Kublai Khan
    c. Genghis Kahn
    d. Mohammed II

13. What did Ahab want Naboth to give him?
    a. His vineyard
    b. His flock of sheep
    c. His wife
    d. His firstborn son

14. Who said "[Russia] is a riddle wrapped in a mystery inside an enigma"?
    a. John Reed
    b. Franklin Roosevelt
    c. Winston Churchill
    d. Nikita Khruschev

15. What did the three branches in the dream represent to Joseph?
    a. Three tribes
    b. Three brothers
    c. Three wise men
    d. Three days

16. Where did the worst aviation disaster in history occur?
    a. Over the ocean between Siberia and Japan
    b. Tenerife, Canary Islands
    c. Chicago
    d. Riyadh, Saudi Arabia

17. What was the first state to ratify the U.S. Constitution?
    a. Massachusetts
    b. Pennsylvania
    c. Delaware
    d. New York

18. Why did King Edward VIII of England abdicate his throne?
    a. To marry a divorcée
    b. To marry a Jewish woman
    c. He suffered a nervous breakdown
    d. He was an alcoholic

19. How did God punish the builders of the Tower of Babel?
    a. He turned them into pillars of salt
    b. He prohibited them from entering the Holy Land
    c. He made them speak different languages
    d. He sent them Twelve Plagues

20. Who ruled over Albania during World War II?
    a. Hitler
    b. Mussolini
    c. King Zog I
    d. King Victor Emmanuel II

21. Which U.S. organization helped secure the prohibition of sales of alcoholic beverages in this country?
    a. National Temperance League
    b. Sherman Antitrust Organization
    c. Anti-Saloon League
    d. U.S. Sobriety Committee

22. What country possessed Angola until its independence in 1975?
    a. Portugal
    b. Cuba
    c. South Africa
    d. Belgium

23. Who were the Jotuns?
    a. Peruvian shrine keepers
    b. Ice monsters
    c. Ancient spiritual healers
    d. Hindu godhead

24. What was "Operation Barbarossa" in World War II?
    a. The code name for D-Day
    b. The code name for the British invasion of the Dardanelles
    c. The failed German invasion of the Soviet Union
    d. The first American attack on Japan

25. Who was the father of Judas Maccabaeus?
    a. Jonah
    b. Joseph
    c. Mattathias
    d. Amos

26. Who was the first Prime Minister of Israel?
    a. Chaim Weizmann
    b. David Ben-Gurion
    c. Moshe Dayan
    d. Golda Meir

27. Who was Moses' brother?
    a. Benjamin
    b. David
    c. Daniel
    d. Aaron

28. What document says, "No freeman shall be taken or imprisoned . . . except by the legal judgment of his peers of the law of the land"?
    a. The U.S. Constitution
    b. The Magna Carta
    c. The Emancipation Proclamation
    d. The Constitution of France

29. Who was the wife of Uriah?
    a. Rachel
    b. Jezebel
    c. Deborah
    d. Bathsheba

30. Who said, "We must all hang together, or assuredly we shall all hang separately"?
    a. Benjamin Franklin
    b. George Washington
    c. Robert E. Lee
    d. Frederick Douglass

31. The first representative assembly in the New World was known by what name?
    a. Confederate Assembly
    b. House of Burgesses
    c. Parliament of the Colonies
    d. Continental Congress

32. What were the famous words of William Prescott at the Battle of Bunker Hill?
    a. "Don't one of you fire until you see the whites of their eyes"
    b. "Taxation without representation is tyranny"
    c. "Rascals, would you live forever?"
    d. "What a glorious morning for America"

33. Who was the last of the judges?
    a. Saul
    b. Solomon
    c. Samuel
    d. Michael

34. Who said, "Sic semper tyrannis. The South is avenged!"?
    a. Frederick Douglass
    b. John Wilkes Booth
    c. John C. Calhoun
    d. Jefferson Davis

35. What is the name of the patriarch of western monks?
    a. St. Bernard
    b. St. Dominic
    c. St. Gregory
    d. St. Benedict

36. Who said, "The unleashed power of the atom has changed everything save our modes of thinking, and we thus drift toward unparalleled catastrophes"?
    a. Harry Truman
    b. J. Robert Oppenheimer
    c. Enrico Fermi
    d. Albert Einstein

37. Who was the founder of the Friars Minor?
    a. St. Francis of Assisi
    b. St. Benedict
    c. St. Francis Xavier
    d. St. Peter

38. In what speech did FDR say, "The only thing we have to fear is fear itself"?
    a. War message to Congress, Dec. 8, 1941
    b. Third Inaugural Address
    c. First Inaugural Address
    d. Acceptance speech for the 1932 Democratic nomination

39. Name the very last of the continental United States to enter the union.
    a. Utah
    b. New Mexico
    c. Arizona
    d. Oklahoma

40. Which American President said, "All free men, wherever they may live, are citizens of Berlin"?
    a. Franklin D. Roosevelt
    b. Harry Truman
    c. Dwight Eisenhower
    d. John F. Kennedy

41. In Christian art, what animal symbolized Mark?
    a. Lamb
    b. Serpent
    c. Lion
    d. Cat

42. Who said, "Injustice anywhere is a threat to justice everywhere"?
    a. Thomas Jefferson
    b. Martin Luther King
    c. Earl Warren
    d. Learned Hand

43. Who was the king who ordered the wise men to report on the birth of Jesus?
    a. Solomon
    b. Caesar
    c. Herod
    d. David

44. Where was Princess Elizabeth on the day her father, King George VI, died and she became Queen of England?
    a. Dublin
    b. India
    c. West Indies
    d. Kenya

45. What were the Stoics named after?
    a. Sir George Stokes
    b. Portico in Athens
    c. Temple in Troy
    d. Steps in Thessalonoki

46. Whose assassination foreshadowed World War I?
    a. Archduke Charles of Hungary
    b. Emperor Franz Joseph of Austria
    c. Archduke Francis Ferdinand of Austria
    d. Gavrilo Princip

47. What was the name of Jason's ship?
    a. *Pagasae*
    b. *Helios*
    c. *Ares*
    d. *Argo*

48. Who was Nazi Germany's Minister of Propaganda and Enlightenment?
    a. Hermann Goering
    b. Joseph Goebbels
    c. Ernst Roehm
    d. Adolf Hitler

49. According to Homer, who was the goddess of wisdom?
    a. Athena
    b. Aphrodite
    c. Diana
    d. Hera

50. What was "The Great Leap Forward"?
    a. Harry Truman's re-election platform
    b. Slogan of the American labor movement in the 1920s
    c. Chinese program to modernize the communistic state
    d. Lenin's favorite slogan

51. The followers of Mahavira practice what religion?
    a. Jainism
    b. Zen Buddhism
    c. Hinduism
    d. Mahayanaism

52. Who originated the term "Cold War"?
    a. Winston Churchill
    b. Bernard Baruch
    c. Joseph McCarthy
    d. Josef Stalin

53. The Bhagavad Gita is used as part of what religion?
    a. Sikhism
    b. Buddhism
    c. Hinduism
    d. Unification Church

54. Whose doctrines were the focus of the Chinese "Cultural Revolution"?
    a. Lao-tzu
    b. Confucius
    c. Gandhi
    d. Mao Tse-tung

55. What religion was founded by George Fox?
    a. Unitarian
    b. Presbyterian
    c. Quaker
    d. Methodist

56. What is the Basque town that was destroyed by German bombers on April 27, 1937?
    a. Guernica
    b. Bayonne
    c. Pamplona
    d. Valladolid

57. What is Ram Dass's real name?
    a. Stephen Albert
    b. Albert Stevens
    c. Richard Alpert
    d. Timothy Allen

58. Name the province of the Belgian Congo that declared itself independent, causing a bloody civil war.
    a. Shaba
    b. Lumumba
    c. Katanga
    d. Tshombe

59. What is the ritual bath in the Jewish religion called?
    a. Mitzvah
    b. Hatikva
    c. Hamotze
    d. Mikvah

60. Who was Assistant Secretary of the Navy when President McKinley declared war on Spain?
    a. Theodore Roosevelt
    b. Woodrow Wilson
    c. William Howard Taft
    d. Admiral Dewey

61. Who adopted Esther?
    a. Ahasuerus
    b. Mordecai
    c. Solomon
    d. Moses

62. What did the Kellogg-Briand Pact outlaw?
    a. Arms buildup
    b. Secret diplomacy
    c. Drinking alcohol
    d. War

63. The Dead Sea Scrolls tell about the monastic life of what community?
    a. Maccabees
    b. Essenes
    c. Levites
    d. Philippians

64. Who was nicknamed the "Happy Warrior" by FDR?
    a. George Patton
    b. Harry Truman
    c. Al Smith
    d. Thomas Dewey

65. Who offered to find a nurse for Moses after he was discovered by Pharaoh's daughter?
    a. Ruth
    b. Miriam
    c. Judith
    d. Jochebed

66. Who won the Battle of Trafalgar?
    a. Duke of Wellington

b. Napoleon
c. Lord Nelson
d. George IV

67. In what book of the Bible does it say, "For everything there is a season, and a time for everything under heaven"?
a. The Song of Songs
b. Book of Ecclesiastes
c. Book of Proverbs
d. Book of Psalms

68. Why did two million people leave Ireland between 1845 and 1847?
a. Potato famine
b. Terrorism by Irish Catholic radicals
c. To escape Protestant religious persecution
d. Irish coal mines were depleted

69. What is the name given to the collection of 15 books not included in either the Old or New Testament?
a. Book of Kings and Prophets
b. Book of Psalms
c. Apocrypha
d. Song of Solomon

70. Who accused the early Christians of starting a fire that nearly destroyed Rome?
a. Julius Caesar
b. Caligula
c. Pontius Pilate
d. Nero

71. Who regained control of Mexico from the French?
a. Benito Juárez
b. Antonio López de Santa Anna
c. Porfirio Díaz
d. Anastasio Bustamente

72. What book of the Old Testament contains many moral and ritual laws such as what is and is not kosher?
a. Numbers
b. Deuteronomy
c. Judges
d. Leviticus

73. What was the first capital of the United States?
a. New York
b. Boston
c. Philadelphia
d. Baltimore

74. What religion in the U.S. uses peyote as part of its ritual ceremony?
a. Unification Church
b. People's Temple
c. Native American Church
d. Shakers

75. The colony of Maryland began as a refuge for what religious group?
a. Puritans
b. Roman Catholics
c. Quakers
d. Anglicans

76. The first settlers of Manhattan island were refugee Protestants from the southern provinces of the Netherlands who were known by what name?
a. Flemings
b. Frisians
c. Walloons
d. Anti-Christs

77. What is another title for the "Book of Changes"?
a. The Psalms
b. The Koran
c. The Book of Numbers
d. The I Ching

78. The first printing press in the colonies outside of New England was found in what colony?
a. Virginia
b. New York
c. Georgia
d. Pennsylvania

79. Who founded the Mormon Church?
a. Brigham Young
b. Joseph Smith
c. John Smythe
d. John Smith

80. Which of the following was *not* one of the original 13 colonies?
a. New Hampshire
b. Georgia
c. Vermont
d. Delaware

81. Which church was founded by John Calvin?
a. Episcopalian
b. Methodist
c. Baptist
d. Presbyterian

82. In 1831 William Lloyd Garrison published a paper based on the principle that slavery was wrong, and the paper was called by what name?
a. *The Freedom Journal*
b. *The Boston Free Gazette*
c. *The Liberator*
d. *The Conscience of the North*

83. What American religious group settled in Germantown, Pennsylvania?
    a. The Mennonites
    b. The Shakers
    c. The Quakers
    d. The Lutherans

84. The political party known as the Whigs was formed almost singlehandedly by whom?
    a. Martin Van Buren
    b. Henry Clay
    c. James Polk
    d. James Buchanan

85. What religious group was founded by Charles T. Russell?
    a. Jehovah's Witnesses
    b. United Church of God
    c. The Assembly of God
    d. Baptists

86. How much did the Louisiana Purchase cost?
    a. $1.5 million
    b. $50 million
    c. $15 million
    d. $750,000

87. Name the Jewish Festival of Booths.
    a. Purim
    b. Simcha Torah
    c. Chanukah
    d. Succoth

88. "The Star-Spangled Banner" was written by Francis Scott Key during the bombardment of what fort?
    a. Fort Sumter
    b. Fort McHenry
    c. Fort Dúquesne
    d. Fort Clay

89. What religious group was founded on the denial that there are three persons in one God?
    a. The Unitarians
    b. The Congregationalists
    c. The Society of Friends
    d. The Christian Reformed Church

90. Who was the first American speculator to settle in then Mexican Texas?
    a. Sam Houston
    b. Jacob Galveston
    c. Stephen Austin
    d. Davy Crockett

91. Who had the shortest reign of any pope?
    a. John XXIII
    b. Paul VI
    c. John Paul I
    d. John Paul II

92. Who was known as the "Little Giant"?
    a. Stephen Douglas
    b. Napoleon
    c. Millard Fillmore
    d. Mussolini

93. Where were the Three Taverns located?
    a. Via Dolorosa
    b. Via Appia
    c. Bethlehem
    d. Gethsemane

94. In what town was the transcontinental railway completed?
    a. Sante Fe, New Mexico
    b. Atchison, Kansas
    c. Promontory Point, Utah
    d. Reno, Nevada

95. What is an enclosed area of a monastery called?
    a. Grisaille
    b. Chapel
    c. Transept
    d. Cloister

96. What was the capital city of the Confederacy?
    a. Atlanta
    b. Durham
    c. New Orleans
    d. Richmond

97. Which Apostle carries a set of keys?
    a. St. Peter
    b. St. Andrew
    c. St. James
    d. St. Paul

98. Who was the founder of Alabama's Tuskegee Institute?
    a. George Washington Carver
    b. Booker T. Washington
    c. W.E.B. Du Bois
    d. Frederick Douglass

99. In iconography, what is the name of a cross on three steps?
    a. Cross-Fleury
    b. St. Andrew's Cross
    c. The Jerusalem Cross
    d. Calvary Cross

100. Name the first independent Latin American country.
    a. Mexico
    b. Haiti
    c. Brazil
    d. Peru

Answers

1. **C** Worms. In 1521, the Edict of Worms forbade anyone to read anything by Luther.

2. **D** Cheops. Built between 2650 and 2500 B.C., the pyramid is 450 feet high and weighs 4,883,000 tons. Building the pyramids left Egypt economically devastated for decades.

3. **B** The Imitation of Christ. It was the literary product of a group in Holland called the Brethren of the Common Life and was written in the Middle Ages.

4. **D** Saul. He was killed by the Philistines and was succeeded by David circa 1000 B.C.

5. **D** John Huss. He came from Bohemia and led an enormous religious revolt.

6. **B** Pericles. The Age of Pericles (c.460–429 B.C.) was a high mark for Greek art, science and democracy.

7. **A** Throne. Cathedrals in large towns were the seat of a bishop's throne.

8. **B** Leif Ericsson. He explored the coast of New England around A.D. 1000.

9. **D** Gregory VII. Known as the Hildebrand, he also ordered the Emperor of Germany to accept the idea that bishops were to receive their instructions from the Pope and not from him, the Emperor.

10. **C** Florence. It was the center of the early Renaissance due in large part to the leadership and patronage of the powerful and wealthy Medici family.

11. **C** The Mount of Olives. Located near Jerusalem, it was here that Jesus said he had to return to his Father, but that his teachings would live forever.

12. **C** Genghis Khan. As a teenager, he founded the Mongolian Empire, which later grew to 10 million square miles, including Eastern Europe, Russia and China.

13. **A** His vineyard. Ahab's wife, Jezebel, plotted to have Naboth stoned to death. She was subsequently murdered and eaten by dogs.

14. **C** Winston Churchill. These remarks, made in a speech on October 1, 1939, were in response to Russia's allying with Nazi Germany and seizing East Poland in September 1939.

15. **D** Three days. He foretold that in three days the Pharaoh would release a fellow prisoner.

16. **B** Tenerife, Canary Islands. A Pan Am 747 and a KLM 747 collided, killing 581 people on March 27, 1977.

17. **C** Delaware. By a unanimous vote, the state ratified the nation's constitution on December 7, 1787. Pennsylvania was the second state to ratify and New Jersey was the third.

18. **A** To marry a divorcée. His wife-to-be, Mrs. Wallis Simpson, had been divorced twice, and such a marriage was considered highly improper for the King, who was also Supreme Governor of the Church of England.

19. **C** He made them speak different languages. The builders then dispersed because they couldn't understand one another and the tower was never finished.

20. **D** King Victor Emmanuel II. Because of Mussolini's occupation of Albania and the exile of King Zog I, the Italian King could do this as well as rule over Ethiopia.

21. **C** Anti-Saloon League. Founded in 1893, it lobbied for the 18th Amendment establishing Prohibition.

22. **A** Portugal. Angola had been a Portuguese colony since 1575.

23. **B** Ice Monsters. They were prominent in Norse mythology and came from Jotunheim.

24. **C** The failed German invasion of the Soviet Union. Occurring in 1941, it was the largest military operation in history.

25. **C** Mattathias. He was a high priest, and after he acquired the name of Maccabaeus, the family and their followers became known as Maccabaeans.

26. **B** David Ben-Gurion. He served from 1948 to 1953 and again from 1955 until 1963.

27. **D** Aaron. He was three years older than Moses, and he was the son of Amram and Jochebed of the Levi tribe.

28. **B** The Magna Carta. In 1215, the barons of England forced King John to sign this document.

29. **D** Bathsheba. She made love to David while still married and married David after her husband was killed on a dangerous mission.

30. **A** Benjamin Franklin. He said this at the signing of the Declaration of Independence on July 4, 1776.

31. **B** House of Burgesses. This assembly was elected July 30, 1619 at Jamestown, Virginia.

32. **A** "Don't one of you fire until you see the whites of their eyes." This important battle was actually fought on nearby Breed's Hill.

33. **C** Samuel. He was the most dominant of these leaders who believed they had direct access to the Lord and who influenced the tribes of Israel.

34. **B** John Wilkes Booth. He uttered these words after shooting President Lincoln.

35. **D** Benedict. He combined a belief in discipline with a respect for human personality and individual capabilities.

36. **D** Albert Einstein. For his work in theoretical physics, notably on the photoelectric effect, he received the 1921 Nobel Prize in physics.

37. **A** St. Francis of Assisi. His order of friars, the Franciscans, was pledged to poverty and scholarship.

38. **C** First Inaugural Address. Given on March 4, 1933, the speech attempted to allay the country's worst fears of the Depression.

39. **C** Arizona. Even though the state's first European settlement occurred in 1776, Arizona was not admitted to the union until Feb. 14, 1912.

40. **D** John F. Kennedy. He said these words in a 1963 speech in West Berlin, and his phrase "Ich bin ein Berliner" won the hearts of all free people.

41. **C** The lion. This particular lion carries with it a feeling of energy, strength and love.

42. **B** Martin Luther King. He wrote this in a letter in a Birmingham, Alabama, jail in August 1963.

43. **C** Herod. Herod told the Wise Men that he too wanted to go and worship him, but happily, the Wise Men did not return to Herod.

44. **D** Kenya. It was February 6, 1952, while she was on a holiday.

45. **B** Portico in Athens. The Stoa Poikile was where Zeno taught his philosophy that man is happy when he does not want things to be other than they are.

46. **C** Archduke Francis Ferdinand of Austria. Because he was killed by a Serbian student, Gavrilo Princip in Sarajevo on June 28, 1914, war broke out between Austria-Hungary and Serbia a month later, which led to World War I.

47. **D** *Argo.* He piloted this boat while searching for the Golden Fleece.

48. **B** Joseph Goebbels. He killed himself, his wife, and his six children in Hitler's bunker the day after Hitler and Eva Braun committed suicide there.

49. **A** Athena. This daughter of Zeus was born by springing out of Zeus' head.

50. **C** Chinese program to modernize the communistic state. Massive agricultural communes were created between 1958 and 1961, but they failed because of natural disasters and poor management.

51. **A** Jainism. The Jains of India believe that all knowledge is relative and transient and that one may answer yes and no to every question.

52. **B** Bernard Baruch. Besides being an economic adviser to the government during both world wars, Baruch was also a confidant of American presidents.

53. **C** Hinduism. The holy book has influenced Hindu holy men for 2000 years.

54. **D** Mao Tse-tung. The Cultural Revolution from 1965 to 1968 was a conservative back-

lash against Soviet influences and liberal trends in the Chinese Communist Party.

55. **C** Quaker. Also known as The Society of Friends, they believe that every person has the potential to be a spokesman of God.

56. **A** Guernica. The destruction of this town in northeast Spain on April 27, 1937, is depicted in Picasso's most famous painting.

57. **C** Richard Alpert. He was connected with Timothy Leary in the sixties, and he now runs a spiritual foundation in New Mexico.

58. **C** Katanga. The copper-rich province rejoined the republic in 1963. The country is now known as Zaire.

59. **D** Mikvah. Devout Jewish women are required to bathe in the Mikvah before the Sabbath.

60. **A** Theodore Roosevelt. He resigned his post to form the Rough Riders cavalry unit in the Spanish-American War.

61. **B** Mordecai. Later, Esther was chosen by King Ahasuerus to be his queen.

62. **D** War. Proposed by French Foreign Minister Briand and expanded by U.S. Secretary of State Kellogg, this nonaggression pact was endorsed in 1928 by sixty nations including Germany and the USSR.

63. **B** Essenes. Discovered in 1947 in Qumran, the scrolls described this Jewish sect which flourished two centuries before Christ.

64. **C** Al Smith. He was Governor of New York and the 1928 Democratic Presidential candidate who lost to Herbert Hoover.

65. **B** Miriam. She was Moses' sister who brought their mother to nurse the child.

66. **C** Lord Nelson. Commanding the British navy, he defeated the combined French and Spanish fleets in the Strait of Gibraltar.

67. **B** The Book of Ecclesiastes. Ecclesiastes was a preacher addressing his congregation, although the book was thought to have been written by King Solomon.

68. **A** Potato famine. Between the famine and a typhus epidemic, over 750,000 people died.

69. **C** The Apocrypha. It was written in the last two centuries B.C. and first century A.D. and not included in the Hebrew canon of the Bible.

70. **D** Nero. In A.D. 64, Christians were unpopular because they worshiped someone who had been crucified by the Romans.

71. **A** Benito Juárez. He was President of Mexico before and after the reign of the French puppet, Emperor Maximilian.

72. **D** Leviticus. This book of laws also tells of the sacred festivals and mentions "Eye for eye."

73. **A** New York. Washington, D.C., wasn't used as the capital until 1800, although its site was picked in 1790.

74. **C** Native American Church. Members combine peyote experiences with Christianity.

75. **B** Roman Catholics. It was founded by Cecilius, son of George Calvert, Lord Baltimore.

76. **C** Walloons. Thirty families settled there in 1623 under the auspices of the Dutch West India Company.

77. **D** The I Ching. The book explains the 64 hexagrams. By picking at random 2 of the 64 hexagrams, one can interpret the changes in the lines, which is a technique of divination.

78. **D** Pennsylvania. The colony was known for its high cultural level, its libraries, refined homes, and interest in science.

79. **B** Joseph Smith. He did it after receiving a series of divine communications.

80. **C** Vermont. From 1781 until 1791, Vermont functioned as a sovereign state before joining the Union.

81. **D** Presbyterian. Calvin believed in duty and self-discipline and changed the mood of the citizens of Geneva to a puritanical self-righteousness.

82. **C** *The Liberator*. Two years later, Garrison formed the American Anti-Slavery Society, which helped to cement Northern antislavery sentiment.

83. **A** The Mennonites. They arrived from Krefeld, Germany, in 1683.

84. **B** Henry Clay. This statesman ran unsuccessfully for the Presidency twice and was known as the Great Compromiser.

85. **A** Jehovah's Witnesses. Founded in 1872, the group was also known as the "Russellites."

86. **C** $15 million. With his armies decimated by yellow fever, Napoleon sold the territory to finance his wars in Europe.

87. **D**   Succoth. After the harvest, all Israelites were required to live in a booth made of palm fronds and boughs of trees.

88. **B**   Fort McHenry. He wrote it on September 13 and 14, 1814, while the British were hammering at the fort.

89. **A**   The Unitarians. They believe that Christ is both human and divine.

90. **C**   Stephen Austin. In 1821, Austin received a grant to settle 300 families on the Colorado River.

91. **C**   John Paul I. He died after thirty-four days in the Vatican.

92. **A**   Stephen Douglas. He was Lincoln's opponent in the Lincoln-Douglas debates.

93. **B**   On the Via Appia (the Appian Way). When Paul was on his way to Rome, Christians came out of the city and met him there.

94. **C**   Promontory Point, Utah. It was here that they drove the golden spike to commemorate the completion.

95. **D**   Cloister. Used mainly as a meeting place for monks, they were sometimes divided and made into small studies used for writing or copying.

96. **D**   Richmond, Virginia. After several Union assaults, the city fell to General Grant and was burned in April 1865.

97. **A**   St. Peter. According to St. Peter, Christ gave him the keys to the Kingdom of Heaven.

98. **B**   Booker T. Washington. A renowned black educator, he was the son of a slave. His autobiography was entitled *Up From Slavery*.

99. **D**   Calvary Cross. The steps symbolize the three graces: faith, hope and charity.

100. **B**   Haiti. A former slave, Toussaint L'Ouverture, led his people to independence in 1800.

FOUR

Entertainment

(Movies, Pop Music, Television, Radio, Theater, Dance)

1. For what group did Richard Starkey play?
   a. The Rolling Stones
   b. The Beatles
   c. The Who
   d. The Kinks

2. The Cole Porter musical *Kiss Me Kate* is an adaptation of which Shakespeare comedy?
   a. *Twelfth Night*
   b. *A Midsummer Night's Dream*
   c. *The Taming of the Shrew*
   d. *Love's Labour's Lost*

3. In Fellini's *Nights of Cabiria*, what is Cabiria's profession?
   a. Cabdriver
   b. Housewife
   c. Actress
   d. Prostitute

4. What successful film director flourished in early TV and directed the *Mama* series?
   a. Mel Brooks
   b. Mike Nichols
   c. Sidney Lumet
   d. Richard Benjamin

5. What was the name of the Beatles' first single?
   a. "I Want to Hold Your Hand"
   b. "Love Me Do"
   c. "She Loves Me"
   d. "Please Please Me"

6. In the hit musical *Blossom Time*, Dorothy Donnelly adapted a German operetta based on the life of which composer?
   a. Paul Hindemith
   b. Ludwig van Beethoven
   c. Robert Schumann
   d. Franz Schubert

7. What is the name of the church that causes a great deal of confusion for Doris Day and James Stewart in Hitchcock's *The Man Who Knew Too Much*?
   a. Albert Hall
   b. Westminster Abbey
   c. Ambrose Chapel
   d. Canterbury Cathedral

8. Former chairman of the board of RCA David Sarnoff began his illustrious career in what capacity?
   a. Truck driver
   b. Office boy
   c. Journalist
   d. Page

9. From what commercial does "Music to Watch Girls By" come?
   a. Pepsi
   b. Coke
   c. Alka-Seltzer
   d. 7-Up

10. Name the former football star who played the original lead in *All God's Chillun Got Wings*.
    a. James Earl Jones
    b. Osgood Perkins
    c. O. J. Simpson
    d. Paul Robeson

11. Who was the original choice to play Margo Channing in *All About Eve* before Bette Davis?
    a. Tallulah Bankhead
    b. Joan Crawford
    c. Claudette Colbert
    d. Eleanor Parker

12. Who originally played Riley in *The Life of Riley* on TV?
    a. Art Carney
    b. Jackie Gleason
    c. William Bendix
    d. William Demarest

13. When Florence Ballard left The Supremes in 1967, who replaced her?
    a. Jean Terrell
    b. Cindy Birdsong
    c. Shari Payne
    d. Mary Wilson

14. What play by Maxwell Anderson won the first New York Drama Critics Award in 1935?
    a. *Winterset*
    b. *Summer*
    c. *What Price Glory?*
    d. *Elizabeth the Queen*

15. What movie star was born Marion Michael Morrison and played football for USC?
    a. Tom Selleck
    b. Ward Bond
    c. Ronald Reagan
    d. John Wayne

16. On the famous children's TV show, *Kukla, Fran & Ollie*, what was the name of the witch?
    a. Buelah
    b. Fran
    c. Kukla
    d. Matilda

17. Who was the original King of Rock and Roll?
    a. Bill Haley
    b. Alan Freed
    c. Murray the K
    d. Elvis Presley

18. Who designed the set for the ballet *Le Boeuf sur le Toit*, which included a cast of famous clowns and acrobats?
    a. Pablo Picasso
    b. Georges Braque
    c. Salvador Dali
    d. Jean Cocteau

19. What is the name of the actress who portrays Glinda the Good Witch in the film *The Wizard of Oz*?
    a. Margaret Hamilton
    b. Binnie Barnes
    c. Billie Burke
    d. Jeanette MacDonald

20. What was the original name of *The Ed Sullivan Show*?
    a. *Front Page*
    b. *Center Ring*
    c. *Toast of the Town*
    d. *Out and About*

21. Where was the Beatles' final concert?
    a. Los Angeles
    b. Chicago
    c. London
    d. San Francisco

22. In Merce Cunningham's modern dance *Winterbranch*, whose music was used as accompaniment?
    a. Robert Schumann

b. John Cage
c. Erik Satie
d. Igor Stravinsky

23. United Artists was formed by D. W. Griffith, Douglas Fairbanks, Charles Chaplin, and what queen of silent films?
    a. Clara Bow
    b. Norma Talmadge
    c. Lillian Gish
    d. Mary Pickford

24. The host of the remake of *You Bet Your Life* was which popular personality?
    a. George Carlin
    b. Richard Dawson
    c. Buddy Hackett
    d. Bill Cullen

25. What was Motown's first record to hit number one on the pop charts?
    a. "I'll Be There"
    b. "Baby Love"
    c. "Please Mr. Postman"
    d. "Shop Around"

26. Which song was in the Broadway musical *Bye Bye Birdie*, but was omitted from the movie?
    a. "Tomorrow"
    b. "Kids"
    c. "An English Teacher"
    d. "Joey"

27. Hurt by the criticism that he was a racist, D. W. Griffith made what film as a response?
    a. *The Birth of a Nation*
    b. *Judith of Bethulia*
    c. *Intolerance*
    d. *Broken Blossoms*

28. The American Broadcasting Company started out in what capacity?
    a. A local midwest TV station
    b. An early film company
    c. A telegraph company
    d. An NBC subsidiary

29. Who was the most outspoken opponent of rock and roll in the 1950s?
    a. Lawrence Welk
    b. Jimmy Dodd
    c. Arthur Godfrey
    d. Mitch Miller

30. In what capacity on Broadway did Jo Mielziner gain fame?
    a. Director
    b. Producer
    c. Set designer
    d. Costume designer

31. What was Grace Kelly's first film?
    a. *Fourteen Hours*
    b. *High Noon*
    c. *Mogambo*
    d. *Green Fire*

32. What is the main business of the A. C. Nielsen Company?
    a. Food reports
    b. TV ratings
    c. Political surveys
    d. Tax returns

33. If you remember this pop music hit, why did the Flying Purple People Eater come to earth?
    a. To eat people
    b. To get a job
    c. To dance
    d. To make friends

34. The character Sheridan Whiteside in *The Man Who Came to Dinner* was supposedly based on whom?
    a. George S. Kaufman
    b. H. L. Mencken
    c. Alexander Woollcott
    d. Fiorello LaGuardia

35. In what musical film does Fred Astaire dance on the walls and the ceiling?
    a. *Shall We Dance?*
    b. *Royal Wedding*
    c. *The Belle of New York*
    d. *Daddy Long Legs*

36. The popular radio characters of Fibber McGee and Molly were played by whom?
    a. Jim and Marion Jordan
    b. Orin Tucker and Bonnie Baker
    c. Kay Kyser and Ginny Simms
    d. Janet Gaynor and Charles Farrell

37. What was Phil Spector's first million-record seller?
    a. "I Love How You Love Me"
    b. "Corrina Corrina"
    c. "Be My Baby"
    d. "To Know Him Is to Love Him"

38. What was the name of the Broadway organization founded by Harold Clurman, Lee Strasberg and Cheryl Crawford?
    a. The Group Theatre
    b. Lincoln Center
    c. Actor's Equity
    d. The Actor's Fund

39. Barbra Streisand played the Katharine Hepburn role in the remake of what Hepburn–Cary Grant comedy?
    a. *The Owl and the Pussycat*
    b. *The Philadelphia Story*
    c. *Bringing Up Baby*
    d. *For Pete's Sake*

40. The radio series *Hollywood Hotel* was hosted by what well-known personality?
    a. Louella Parsons
    b. George Burns
    c. Hedda Hopper
    d. Will Rogers

41. Who sang the title song in the motion picture *Alfie*?
    a. Dionne Warwick
    b. Cilla Black
    c. Cher
    d. Shirley Bassey

42. Which of the following Broadway couples doesn't belong in the group?
    a. Jessica Tandy and Hume Cronyn
    b. Helen Hayes and Charles MacArthur
    c. Betty Comden and Adolph Green
    d. Anne Jackson and Eli Wallach

43. Frederic Raphael, the screenwriter for *Darling*, wrote the innovative screenplay for what Stanley Donen/Audrey Hepburn project?
    a. *The Nun's Story*
    b. *Two for the Road*
    c. *Wait Until Dark*
    d. *Robin and Marion*

44. Frank Sinatra got his first regular job on what radio show?
    a. *The Fred Allen Show*
    b. *The Stage Door Canteen*
    c. *Grand Ole Opry*
    d. *The Jimmy Durante Show*

45. What pop singer's real name is David Jones?
    a. Quincy Jones
    b. David Crosby
    c. Brian Jones
    d. David Bowie

46. What was Neil Simon's first Broadway hit?
    a. *Gingerbread Lady*
    b. *Barefoot in the Park*
    c. *The Odd Couple*
    d. *Come Blow Your Horn*

47. What popular actress of the 50s and 60s plays Anne, the woman who provokes Jean Seberg's jealousy in *Bonjour Tristesse*?
    a. Gina Lollobrigida
    b. Rita Hayworth
    c. Deborah Kerr
    d. Dorothy McGuire

48. What actor played Sam Spade on the radio?
    a. Humphrey Bogart
    b. Ronald Coleman
    c. Howard Duff
    d. Sonny Tufts

49. What was the first pop album to sell a million copies?
    a. *Whole Lot of Shakin' Going On*
    b. *Calypso*
    c. *Connie Francis' Greatest Hits*
    d. *Meet the Beatles*

50. What playwright wrote the classic *Volpone*?
    a. William Shakespeare
    b. Cervantes
    c. Molière
    d. Ben Jonson

51. What Akira Kurosawa film is based on Shakespeare's *Macbeth*?
    a. *Rashomon*
    b. *Throne of Blood*
    c. *Ikiru*
    d. *The Seven Samurai*

52. Who played the role of Baby Snooks on the popular radio show?
    a. Fanny Brice
    b. Joan Davis
    c. Gracie Allen
    d. Selma Diamond

53. What pop singing group was sued because of its name?
    a. The Beatles
    b. The Hollies
    c. Chicago
    d. Jefferson Airplane

54. Generally, who is considered the "father of the classic ballet"?
    a. George Balanchine
    b. Marius Petipa
    c. Michail Fokine
    d. Sergei Diaghilev

55. Maureen O'Sullivan, remembered for her role as Jane in the *Tarzan* series of films, is the mother of what other actress?
    a. Anne Archer
    b. Geraldine Chaplin
    c. Tish Sterling
    d. Mia Farrow

56. The NBC Symphony Orchestra played weekly radio concerts for years under the baton of what conductor?
    a. Dimitri Shoshtakovich
    b. Arturo Toscanini
    c. Leonard Bernstein
    d. Ignace Paderewski

57. What New Wave singing group has appeared in a jeans commercial?
    a. Devo
    b. B-52s
    c. Blondie
    d. The Clash

58. Who was choreographer of the ballet *Rodeo*?
    a. Edward Villella
    b. Twyla Tharp
    c. Agnes de Mille
    d. Rudolf Nureyev

59. In what film does James Cagney declare, "Look, Ma, I'm on top of the world!" shortly before he is blown up?
    a. *Public Enemy*
    b. *The Roaring Twenties*
    c. *Angels with Dirty Faces*
    d. *White Heat*

60. Who hosts radio's *America's Top Forty*, which is a rundown of top pop music hits?
    a. Dr. Demento
    b. Larry King
    c. Casey Kasem
    d. Dick Clark

61. Who was the first host of TV's *Midnight Special*?
    a. Don Kirshner
    b. John Denver
    c. Johnny Cash
    d. Lou Rawls

62. What was the name of the dancing done by Loie Fuller with yards of luminous veils?
    a. Fan dancing
    b. Tango
    c. Skirt dancing
    d. Court dancing

63. Hedwige Kiesler is the real name of what movie sex goddess of the 1940s?
    a. Ingrid Bergman
    b. Linda Darnell
    c. Veronica Lake
    d. Hedy Lamarr

64. What was the name of Mary Hartman's father on the popular TV series?
    a. Merle Jeeter
    b. George Shumway
    c. Charlie Haggers
    d. George Hartman

65. What famous singer/composer trained as a hair-dresser?
   a. Andy Gibb
   b. Jerry Lee Lewis
   c. Paul McCartney
   d. Chuck Berry

66. What is the name of the black swan in the popular ballet *Swan Lake*?
   a. Odette
   b. Odile
   c. Arabella
   d. Olympia

67. Films from the 1940s and 1950s, shot in moody black and white, with amoral, tough, criminal characters, are described as films in what genre?
   a. Caper
   b. Gangster
   c. Film Noir
   d. Crime

68. What was the occupation of Fred MacMurray's character on the long-running TV series *My Three Sons*?
   a. Aviation engineer
   b. Hollywood attorney
   c. Advertising executive
   d. Insurance broker

69. Who did the painting on the cover of "Crosby, Stills, Nash and Young's Greatest Hits" album?
   a. Andy Warhol
   b. Judy Collins
   c. Joni Mitchell
   d. Robert Rauschenberg

70. Occupying a famous role in ballet history, Sergei Diaghilev was engaged in what profession?
   a. Dancer
   b. Impresario
   c. Choreographer
   d. Composer

71. What vintage film star was known as the "It" girl?
   a. Ann Sheridan
   b. Joan Crawford
   c. Clara Bow
   d. Gloria DeHaven

72. What is the name of the actor who played Captain Kangaroo on the children's TV series of the same name?
   a. Pinky Lee
   b. Bob Keeshan
   c. Keenan Wynn
   d. Soupy Sales

73. What is Aretha Franklin's only number one hit song?
   a. "You're All I Need to Get By"
   b. "A Natural Woman"
   c. "Mockingbird"
   d. "Respect"

74. What was the name of George M. Cohan's first success on Broadway?
   a. *Hot Tamale Alley*
   b. *The Governor's Son*
   c. *Hiawatha*
   d. *I Guess I'll Have to Telegraph My Baby*

75. What does Terry Malloy, played by Marlon Brando, keep on his rooftop in *On the Waterfront*?
   a. Liquor
   b. Guns
   c. Pigeons
   d. Money

76. What was the name of the girl with dark braids who was a "goody-two shoes" in Beaver's class on TV's *Leave It to Beaver*?
   a. Judy Rutherford
   b. Violet Rutherford
   c. Penny Woods
   d. Judy Hensler

77. According to the hit record "The Shoop Shoop Song," where was "it?"
   a. In his look
   b. In his eyes
   c. In his kiss
   d. In his hug

78. What is the name of the play by George Bernard Shaw about a woman whose income is earned from houses of prostitution?
   a. *Major Barbara*
   b. *Mrs. Warren's Profession*
   c. *Candida*
   d. *How He Lied to Her Husband*

79. The negative of what hugely successful film is stored in a golden canister?
   a. *E.T.*
   b. *Star Wars*
   c. *Jaws*
   d. *Gone With the Wind*

80. Who was television's J. Fred Muggs?
   a. Riley's boss at the plant
   b. Fred Flintstone's neighbor
   c. A regular on *Your Show of Shows*
   d. A monkey on the *Today Show*

81. What pop singer plays a guitar named "Lucille"?
   a. B. B. King
   b. Chuck Berry
   c. Kenny Rogers
   d. Eric Clapton

82. What is the title of the first full-length play written by Eugene O'Neill?
   a. *The Emperor Jones*
   b. *Beyond the Horizon*
   c. *The Hairy Ape*
   d. *Masses and Men*

83. Name Greta Garbo's first "talkie."
   a. *Grand Hotel*
   b. *Queen Christina*
   c. *Anna Christie*
   d. *Anna Karenina*

84. What was the name of the TV show about a family of five—but only two of them were human beings?
   a. *World of Mr. Sweeney*
   b. *The Hathaways*
   c. *Gentle Ben*
   d. *Leave It to Larry*

85. What singer is billed as "Trash With Flash"?
   a. Diana Ross
   b. Alice Cooper
   c. Bette Midler
   d. Gary Glitter

86. What is the name of the hit song of the Broadway musical *Runnin' Wild*, which started a national dance craze in 1923?
   a. "The Black Bottom"
   b. "Charleston"
   c. "Castle Walk"
   d. "Beer Barrel Polka"

87. Who woos Deborah Kerr aboard an ocean liner in *An Affair to Remember*?
   a. Robert Mitchum
   b. David Niven
   c. Rock Hudson
   d. Cary Grant

88. Dean Martin and Jerry Lewis made their television debut on what show?
   a. *The Toast of the Town*
   b. *Colgate Comedy Hour*
   c. *Jack Benny Show*
   d. *Texaco Star Theatre*

89. Who was the first female country star to receive a platinum record?
   a. Dolly Parton
   b. Loretta Lynn

   c. Patsy Cline
   d. Tammy Wynette

90. The famous musical drama *Show Boat*, which made its debut at New York's Ziegfeld Theatre, was based on a book written by what American author?
   a. Lillian Hellman
   b. Willa Cather
   c. Edna Ferber
   d. Doris Lessing

91. When Greer Garson met her future husband, Richard Ney, during the shooting of *Mrs. Miniver*, what role was Ney playing in the film?
   a. Her husband
   b. Her boyfriend
   c. A Nazi soldier
   d. Her son

92. Who was the narrator of TV's *The Untouchables*?
   a. Robert Stack
   b. Ed McMahon
   c. Walter Winchell
   d. Herschel Bernardi

93. Who was the first American singer to record a Beatles' song?
   a. Elvis Presley
   b. Del Shannon
   c. Billy Preston
   d. Judy Collins

94. The haunting song "Someday I'll Find You" is from what play by Noel Coward?
   a. *Blithe Spirit*
   b. *Bittersweet*
   c. *Private Lives*
   d. *The Green Pastures*

95. What film has won more Oscars than any other in history?
   a. *All About Eve*
   b. *Ben Hur*
   c. *The Sound of Music*
   d. *Star Wars*

96. For three years Burt Reynolds co-starred on which western TV series?
   a. *Wagon Train*
   b. *Wanted: Dead or Alive*
   c. *The Rifleman*
   d. *Gunsmoke*

97. Where does the pop group Duran Duran get its name?
   a. Candy bar
   b. African city

c. Law firm
d. Motion picture

98. Sydney Aaron, credited screenwriter of *Altered States*, is the pseudonym for what writer?
    a. Robert Towne
    b. Bo Goldman
    c. Paddy Chayefsky
    d. Philip Dunne

99. Who was the original host of *The Tonight Show*?
    a. Jack Paar

b. Steve Allen
c. Sid Caesar
d. Merv Griffin

100. Who sings the hit song "I Can't Go for That (No Can Do)"?
    a. Steely Dan
    b. Human League
    c. Hall and Oates
    d. Diana Ross

Answers

1. **B** The Beatles. Richard Starkey is Ringo's real name.

2. **C** *The Taming of the Shrew*. Shakespeare wrote this comedy in the 1590s.

3. **D** Prostitute. The role was played by Giulietta Masina.

4. **C** Sidney Lumet. Among the notable TV shows directed by him were *Omnibus* and *You Are There*.

5. **B** "Love Me Do." It was released in October 1962. "I Want to Hold Your Hand," which carried them to international stardom, was not released until late 1963.

6. **D** Franz Schubert. The musical earned its composer, Sigmund Romberg, two thousand times what Schubert earned from all of his compositions.

7. **C** Ambrose Chapel. When this name is passed on to them by a dying spy, Day and Stewart first think it's the name of a man, not a place.

8. **B** Office boy. Starting with American Marconi, he soon became a telegraph operator.

9. **A** Pepsi. It was a big hit for the Bob Crewe Generation.

10. **D** Paul Robeson. Robeson played football for Rutgers. The play was threatened with violence before its opening because of its theme of interracial marriage.

11. **C** Claudette Colbert. She had to bow out of the part because of a back ailment.

12. **B** Jackie Gleason. For only one season in 1949, Gleason starred with Rosemary DeCamp. The show won an Emmy for that year.

13. **B** Cindy Birdsong. Cindy was formerly with Patti LaBelle and the Blue Belles.

14. **A** *Winterset*. The play used the Sacco-Vanzetti case as background.

15. **D** John Wayne. He changed his name when he became a B-western star in the 1930s.

16. **A** Buelah. Some of the show's other characters were Dolores Dragon, Madame Ophelia Oglepuss and Fletcher Rabbit. Burr Tillstrom was the puppeteer on this show, which ran from 1948 until 1957.

17. **B** Alan Freed. He was the influential 1950s disc jockey who is credited with coining the phrase "rock and roll."

18. **D** Jean Cocteau. Incredibly versatile, he produced poetry, fiction, drama, films, ballets, drawings and opera librettos.

19. **C** Billie Burke. She was also known as Mrs. Florenz Ziegfeld.

20. **C** *Toast of the Town*. Launched in 1948, this CBS variety program later changed its name to *The Ed Sullivan Show* and ran until 1971.

21. **D** San Francisco. It was never billed as their farewell concert. They just never performed live together after that.

22. **B** John Cage. The dance was full of frightening and oppressing images. It was choreographed in 1964, at the beginning of the Vietnam War.

23. **D** Mary Pickford. She was married to Fairbanks the following year.

24. **C** Buddy Hackett. Flopping after one short season, the show had been a vehicle for Groucho Marx and was lifeless without him.

25. **C** "Please Mr. Postman." It was sung by the Marvelettes and was Motown's first crossover hit from the R&B charts.

26. **C** "An English Teacher." In the musical, which was directed and choreographed by Gower Champion, Chita Rivera sang this lament.

27. **C** *Intolerance*. Lasting 3¼ hours, the film was a costly bomb for its director.

28. **D** An NBC subsidiary. It was the Blue Network, but NBC was forced to sell it in 1943, and Edward J. Noble, head of Life Savers Corporation, bought it. The network later merged with Paramount Theatres under the aegis of Leonard Goldenson.

29. **D** Mitch Miller. He was head of Columbia Records at the time and went on national television to denounce it. He later lost his job because of his miscalculation.

30. **C** Set designer. Among the more than 200 productions for which he designed the sets were *Death of a Salesman, A Streetcar Named Desire* and *Annie Get Your Gun.*

31. **A** *Fourteen Hours.* This 1951 suspense film about a man threatening to throw himself off a building starred Paul Douglas.

32. **A** Food reports. It was founded in the 1920s and tabulates and reports consumer consumption of drug and food items from retail shelves. Its TV rating activity accounts for 10 percent of its revenues.

33. **B** To get a job. And not just any job . . . it had to be in rock and roll!

34. **C** Alexander Woollcott. The Kaufman and Hart play debuted in 1939 and also boasted characters with a striking resemblance to Tallulah Bankhead and Harpo Marx.

35. **B** *Royal Wedding.* The 1951 MGM musical included this famous number with a rotating set to achieve the effect.

36. **A** Jim and Marion Jordan. Some of the show's other characters were Gildersleeve, Mayor LaTrivia, the Old Timer and Doc Gamble.

37. **D** "To Know Him Is to Love Him." He was still a teenager when he wrote, produced and performed this number-one record in 1958 with the Teddy Bears.

38. **A** The Group Theatre. Original members were Stella Adler, Morris Carnovsky, Lee J. Cobb and Elia Kazan. It led to the founding of The Actors Studio and the Neighborhood Playhouse.

39. **C** *Bringing Up Baby.* This 1938 comedy was the basis for Peter Bogdanovich's *What's Up, Doc?* starring Streisand and Ryan O'Neal.

40. **A** Louella Parsons. Among the other regulars were Dick Powell, Frances Langford and Ted Fio Rito and his orchestra. The weekly show featured music, interviews with film stars, and adaptations of sequences from their current movies.

41. **C** Cher. Dionne Warwick has the super record hit, but Cher sang it on the sound track.

42. **C** Betty Comden and Adolph Green. They're the only listed couple who aren't husband and wife. They are co-lyricist/writers and have collaborated on *On the Town, Wonderful Town* and *Peter Pan.*

43. **B** *Two for the Road.* It was a brilliant non-chronological study of a crumbling marriage which co-starred Albert Finney.

44. **A** *The Fred Allen Show.* Premiering in October 1932, the show ran for fifteen years and featured characters like Senator Claghorn, Mrs. Nussbaum and Titus Moody.

45. **D** David Bowie. He changed his name because there was already a Davy Jones, who was the lead singer for the Monkees.

46. **D** *Come Blow Your Horn.* It took Simon three years to write it. Prior to that, he wrote for television.

47. **C** Deborah Kerr. In the film, she ultimately dies from an accident that the Seberg character had indirectly caused.

48. **C** Howard Duff. Having a rich and sexy baritone voice to go with Hammett's racy dialogue, Duff went on to a successful film career.

49. **B** *Calypso.* It was recorded by Harry Belafonte in 1957.

50. **D** Ben Jonson. This English poet and playwright was a friend of Shakespeare and generally regarded as the first unofficial poet laureate of Britain.

51. **B** *Throne of Blood.* This 1957 classic starred the perennial Samurai warrior, Toshiro Mifune.

52. **A** Fanny Brice. She was a Ziegfeld Follies star who introduced her Baby Snooks character to radio in the 1920s.

53. **C** Chicago. Once known as the Chicago Transit Authority, they were sued by the ultraconservative mayor of Chicago, Richard Daley, to change their name. Thus it was shortened to Chicago.

54. **B** Marius Petipa. He studied in France and danced with the Paris Opera but is best remembered as the choreographer of the Imperial Ballet in St. Petersburg. His best-known works were *Don Quixote, La Bayadère* and *Sleeping Beauty*.

55. **D** Mia Farrow. Her father was director John Farrow.

56. **B** Arturo Toscanini. Competing with CBS broadcasts of the New York Philharmonic, the NBC Symphony began in 1937 with Toscanini drawing outstanding musicians from all over the world.

57. **C** Blondie. For a short while, Deborah Harry was the spokesperson for Gloria Vanderbilt jeans.

58. **C** Agnes de Mille. With music by Aaron Copland, the ballet was premiered at the Metropolitan Opera House in 1942, with de Mille dancing the part of the cowgirl in the production.

59. **D** *White Heat.* This 1949 feature was one of the first postwar crime films to glamorize the amoral punk.

60. **C** Casey Kasem. The ever-present voice-over king hosts the radio show which is also seen on TV with video versions of the songs.

61. **B** John Denver. It premiered on NBC August 19, 1972.

62. **C** Skirt Dancing. She swathed herself in layers of diaphanous fabrics against a backdrop of colored glass lanterns. Isadora Duncan was greatly influenced by Fuller.

63. **D** Hedy Lamarr. Her nude debut in *Extase* in 1933 made a sensation in Europe.

64. **B** George Shumway. Played by Philip Bruno, George was married to Mary's mother, Martha.

65. **D** Chuck Berry. He holds a degree in cosmetology from Gibbs Beauty College.

66. **B** Odile. With a score by Tchaikovsky, the ballet was first presented at Moscow's Bolshoi Theatre in 1877.

67. **C** Film Noir. The phrase was coined by the French postwar critics.

68. **A** Aviation Engineer. However, he seemed to spend more time raising his three sons and fending off marriage-hungry women.

69. **C** Joni Mitchell. She's a talented artist as well as a singer and has done the artwork on many of her own album covers.

70. **B** Impresario. He was a Russian nobleman who studied law and later became a theatrical impresario. In 1909, he assembled a company of dancers in Paris including Fokine, Pavlova and Nijinsky, dancing mainly Fokine's ballets.

71. **C** Clara Bow. A flapper and vamp of the 1920s silent films, her career fell apart after a succession of scandals.

72. **B** Bob Keeshan. He also played Clarabell in the "Howdy Doody Show."

73. **D** "Respect." It seems that the "First Lady of Soul" should have had more since this was only the second song she ever recorded.

74. **A** *Hot Tamale Alley.* George Michael Cohan wrote this when he was 17.

75. **C** Pigeons. All of the birds are slaughtered when Malloy crosses the Mob in this 1954 Best Picture which costarred Eva Marie Saint.

76. **D** Judy Hensler. She was known for being the perfect student who also reminded Miss Landers whenever she forgot anything.

77. **C** In his kiss. If you were listening to all she said when Betty Everett sang this 1964 hit.

78. **B** *Mrs. Warren's Profession.* When first presented in New York, the performers were said to be acting in an "immoral play."

79. **D** *Gone With the Wind.* Until 1967, it was the most popular film ever made.

80. **D** A monkey on the *Today Show.* He lost his job when he bit someone.

81. **A** B. B. King. It comes from the name of a woman two men were fighting over. They set the hotel, where King was staying, on fire. He has called the guitar he saved from the fire "Lucille" ever since.

82. **B** *Beyond the Horizon.* It won the 1920 Pulitzer Prize for drama.

83. **C** *Anna Christie.* This 1930 classic was also Marie Dressler's comeback film.

84. **B** *The Hathaways.* First telecast in 1961, the show starred the Marquis Chimps as well as Jack Weston and Peggy Cass.

85. **C** Bette Midler. She acquired that billing when she began her career singing in a gay bathhouse.

86. **B** "Charleston." It was written by Cecil Mack and Jimmy Johnston and became the anthem for the Roaring Twenties.

87. **D** Cary Grant. The film was a popular but rather soggy remake of 1939's *Love Affair*.

88. **A** *The Toast of the Town*. The show also hosted the American television debut of the Beatles.

89. **D** Tammy Wynette. She won it for her greatest hits album.

90. **C** Edna Ferber. Helen Morgan starred in the show's 1928 debut with music by Jerome Kern and lyrics by Oscar Hammerstein II.

91. **D** Her son. Garson was only 33 when she played the much older Mrs. Miniver. Walter Pidgeon played Mr. Miniver.

92. **C** Walter Winchell. The show starred Robert Stack as Eliot Ness, featured two or three big shoot-outs per episode, and was considered the most violent show of its time in 1960.

93. **B** Del Shannon. In 1963, he recorded "From Me to You" for Big Top Records.

94. **C** *Private Lives*. The show starred Noel Coward, Gertrude Lawrence and Laurence Olivier in the original cast.

95. **B** *Ben Hur*. In 1959, the film acquired a total of eleven Oscars.

96. **D** *Gunsmoke*. During the seasons of 1962 to 1965, he played "Quint Asper."

97. **D** Motion picture. They are named for the villain in the Jane Fonda film *Barbarella*.

98. **C** Paddy Chayefsky. He was so unhappy with Ken Russell's film version of his screenplay that he insisted a pseudonym be used.

99. **B** Steve Allen. He started with the show when it was a local show in 1953 on WNBC-TV in New York.

100. **C** Hall and Oates. It was an amazing crossover hit going to number one on the Pop, Rhythm and Blues, Adult Contemporary, and Dance Charts.

FIVE

The Arts

(Architecture, Art, Classical Music, Language, Literature, Opera)

1. What was the nationality of the painter El Greco?
   a. Spanish
   b. French
   c. Greek
   d. Flemish

2. How old was Mozart when he wrote his first symphony?
   a. Fourteen
   b. Eighteen
   c. Twelve
   d. Eight

3. Who is the hero of *Watership Down*?
   a. Hazel
   b. Peter
   c. Bigwig
   d. Blackberry

4. Where did the term "Op Art" originate?
   a. Museum of Modern Art
   b. Andy Warhol
   c. *Vogue* magazine
   d. *Time* magazine

5. What important composer of the 19th century played piano in brothels as a child?
   a. Schubert
   b. Berlioz
   c. Brahms
   d. Wagner

6. What was the name of King Arthur's sword?
   a. Eureka
   b. Excalibur
   c. Champion
   d. Stone Cleaver

7. What does *chiaroscuro* mean?
   a. A kind of paint
   b. Marble for sculpture
   c. Light and shade in painting
   d. Name of a 16th-century Italian painter

8. The device of *rubato* is identified with what 19th-century composer for the piano?
   a. Brahms
   b. Beethoven
   c. Schumann
   d. Chopin

9. Who addressed the lines "Do not go gentle into that good night" to his dying father?
   a. Hart Crane
   b. Dylan Thomas
   c. James Dickey
   d. e.e. cummings

10. What modern-day American writer painted much sought-after watercolors?
    a. John Steinbeck
    b. William Faulkner
    c. Lillian Hellman
    d. Henry Miller

11. Beethoven's *Third Symphony*—the *Eroica*—was initially inspired by what figure whom Beethoven later reviled?
    a. Peter the Great
    b. George Washington
    c. Napoleon
    d. J. S. Bach

12. Who is the clergyman-victim in T. S. Eliot's *Murder in the Cathedral*?
    a. Pope Gregory
    b. Father Flynn
    c. Thomas à Becket
    d. Deacon Motherwell

13. *Le Déjeuner sur l'Herbe (Luncheon on the Grass)* was painted by what famous artist?
    a. Monet
    b. Manet
    c. Pissarro
    d. Toulouse-Lautrec

14. What prominent opera composer lived illicitly with one of Franz Liszt's daughters?
    a. Verdi
    b. Puccini
    c. Chopin
    d. Wagner

15. What was the major crop that Thoreau planted in his experimental living by Walden Pond?
    a. Pumpkins
    b. Tomatoes
    c. Beans
    d. Cabbage

16. What French painter was known for his portraits of café people?
    a. Toulouse-Lautrec
    b. Degas
    c. Van Gogh
    d. Gauguin

17. What composer is responsible for "Dried Embryos" and other surrealistically titled works?
    a. Arnold Schoenberg
    b. Erik Satie
    c. Charles Ives
    d. Philip Glass

18. In what mock-heroic ballad do we first encounter the words "slithy" and "mimsy"?
    a. "Jabberwocky"
    b. "Greensleeves"
    c. "Elvira"
    d. "Samson and Delilah"

19. What famous New York exhibition introduced "modern" art to the U.S.?
    a. The Picasso show at the Museum of Modern Art
    b. The 1913 New York Armory Show
    c. The opening of the Whitney Museum
    d. The New York World's Fair of 1939

20. Name the author of the popular novel upon which the opera *La Traviata* is based.
    a. Alexandre Dumas *fils*.
    b. Victor Hugo
    c. George Sand
    d. Honoré de Balzac

21. Who wrote the story of lovely Isabel Archer's devastatingly bad marriage to Gilbert Osmond?
    a. T. S. Eliot
    b. William James
    c. James Joyce
    d. Henry James

22. What is the name of the "ground" applied to a canvas before most painting is done?
    a. Gestalt
    b. Milk
    c. Gesso
    d. Varnish

23. What work was not a critical or public success for Tchaikovsky until after his death?
    a. *The Nutcracker*
    b. *Swan Lake*
    c. *Pathétique Symphony*
    d. *The Sleeping Beauty*

24. In what community was the Great Gatsby's mansion?
    a. West Egg, Long Island
    b. Westport, Connecticut
    c. Great Neck, Long Island
    d. Southampton, Long Island

25. What is the name of the Picasso painting showing the horrors of war?
    a. *Guernica*
    b. *Three Dancers*
    c. *The Rape of Europa*
    d. *Night Fishing*

26. Six concerti grossi make up a famous group of Bach's works which are known by what name?
    a. *The Passions*
    b. *Warsaw Concertos*
    c. *Brandenburg Concertos*
    d. *Concertos in F*

27. What ails the children in the novel *The Turn of the Screw*?
    a. They are blind
    b. They are sick
    c. They've been tortured
    d. They're possessed by spirits

28. What Renaissance painter also was known for detailed sketches of human anatomy?
    a. Botticelli
    b. Leonardo da Vinci
    c. Rembrandt
    d. Ghilberti

29. What opera shocked Parisian audiences in the 1870s because the women performing onstage smoked cigarettes?
    a. *Carmen*
    b. *La Bohème*
    c. *La Traviata*
    d. *Faust*

30. What English writer turned a lonely childhood into the source material for stories of rabbits, bunnies, and puddleducks?
    a. Virginia Woolf
    b. Dorothy Sayers
    c. Gertrude Stein
    d. Beatrix Potter

31. Name the row of windows high up on a wall that are used to bring light into a large building.
    a. Clerestory
    b. Nave

c. Transepts
d. Atrium

32. What Russian composer was also a medical doctor and a professor of chemistry?
    a. Rimsky-Korsakov
    b. Borodin
    c. Tchaikovsky
    d. Glinka

33. What is the word that begins and ends the final chapter of James Joyce's *Ulysses*?
    a. No
    b. Maybe
    c. Yes
    d. Psychosis

34. Hagia Sophia in Istanbul was built originally as what type of edifice?
    a. Early Christian church
    b. Islamic mosque
    c. Jewish temple
    d. Emperor's palace

35. What is the name given to Schumann's *Third Symphony*?
    a. *Spring*
    b. *Jupiter*
    c. *Rhenish*
    d. *Winter Dreams*

36. French novelist Émile Zola grew up in Aix-en-Provence with what Impressionist master?
    a. Monet
    b. Cézanne
    c. Seurat
    d. Manet

37. The giant tabernacle in St. Peter's in Rome was created by what artist?
    a. Michelangelo
    b. Bernini
    c. Raphael
    d. Cellini

38. Composer Bedřich Smetana was a native of what country?
    a. Russia
    b. Spain
    c. Rumania
    d. Bohemia

39. Who created the country-bumpkin art critic Clem Clammidge, who appeared at New England art galleries offering homespun comments on modern art?
    a. Kurt Vonnegut, Jr.
    b. Peter De Vries
    c. Bennett Cerf
    d. F. Scott Fitzgerald

40. What popular present-day artist is known for his prints of active sporting events?
    a. LeRoy Neiman
    b. Georges Rouault
    c. Marc Chagall
    d. Adolph Gottlieb

41. What renowned English composer married his secretary at the age of eighty?
    a. Edward Elgar
    b. Ralph Vaughan Williams
    c. Sir Thomas Beecham
    d. Benjamin Britten

42. What does Anna Wulf, the heroine of *The Golden Notebook* by Doris Lessing, do for a living?
    a. Wait tables
    b. Models clothes
    c. Writes novels
    d. Politician

43. French artist Edgar Degas is most remembered for his paintings of what subject matter?
    a. Ballerinas
    b. Water lilies
    c. Sunflowers
    d. His mother

44. What composer uttered the word "Mozart" as he died?
    a. Salieri
    b. Mahler
    c. Schubert
    d. Haydn

45. Who wrote *The Teachings of Don B.: A Yankee Way of Knowledge*?
    a. Carlos Castaneda
    b. Donald Barthelme
    c. Christopher Isherwood
    d. Isaac Bashevis Singer

46. Françoise Gilot, a painter and the wife of Dr. Jonas Salk, was once the mistress of what famous artist?
    a. Matisse
    b. Picasso
    c. Miró
    d. Dali

47. What is the name of Beethoven's only opera?
    a. *The Marriage of Figaro*
    b. *Leonora*
    c. *The Barber of Seville*
    d. *Fidelio*

48. What writer had his autobiographical novel about his hometown of Archer City, Texas turned into an Academy Award-winning film?
    a. Red Ryder
    b. Larry McMurtry
    c. William Styron
    d. Wilson Harris

49. In art terminology, what does "provenance" mean?
    a. Refers to an artist who has "made it"
    b. The history of a kind of painting
    c. The method by which a work is made
    d. The history of the work since it left the artist's hand

50. What Puccini opera is set in a mining town?
    a. *Gianni Schicchi*
    b. *La Fanciulla del West*
    c. *Le Villi*
    d. *Tosca*

51. What is the title of Aeschylus's tragic trilogy?
    a. *Agamemnon*
    b. *Antigone*
    c. *Oresteia*
    d. *Dionysus Cycle*

52. Georgia O'Keeffe is best known for her paintings of what subject?
    a. Sea
    b. Nudes
    c. Flowers
    d. American Indians

53. Name the piano teacher with whom Beethoven argued and finally parted from in his training as a musician.
    a. Mozart
    b. Haydn
    c. Handel
    d. Bach

54. What is the name of the hero in *Jane Eyre* by Charlotte Brontë?
    a. Branwell
    b. Heathcliffe
    c. Rochester
    d. Gondal

55. Who invented the geodesic dome?
    a. Le Corbusier
    b. Buckminster Fuller
    c. Leonardo da Vinci
    d. Mies van der Rohe

56. The works of Goethe inspired *Faust* and what other opera?
    a. *Egmont*
    b. *Götz von Berlichingen*
    c. *Torquato Tasso*
    d. *Werther*

57. Name the half-Scots poet who wrote *Childe Harold* in the early 1800s.
    a. Keats
    b. Shelley
    c. Lord Byron
    d. Robert Burns

58. The portraits of George Washington that are most familiar were done by what artist?
    a. John Singer Sargent
    b. James McNeill Whistler
    c. Gilbert Stuart
    d. Jacques Louis David

59. What composer wrote a piano concerto specifically for a pianist who had lost his right arm in World War I?
    a. Stravinsky
    b. Ravel
    c. Schoenberg
    d. Debussy

60. "Harry Bailly" was the name of which pilgrim in *The Canterbury Tales*?
    a. The Mule Driver
    b. The Pardoner
    c. The Profane Host
    d. The Summoner

61. The painting *American Gothic* was done by what artist?
    a. Andrew Wyeth
    b. Thomas Hart Benton
    c. Grant Wood
    d. Charles Burchfield

62. What popular opera concerns the story of a clown whose wife is cheating on him?
    a. *Rigoletto*
    b. *I Pagliacci*
    c. *Cavalleria Rusticana*
    d. *Un Ballo in Maschera*

63. What author had Polish as his first language, French as his second, but wrote in English?
    a. Somerset Maugham
    b. Joseph Conrad
    c. Franz Kafka
    d. Gerard Manley Hopkins

64. What other well-known sculpture was created by the sculptor of the famous statue *The Thinker*?
    a. *Winged Victory*
    b. *Balzac*
    c. *Cleopatra's Needle*
    d. *Man and Universe*

65. *Mikrokosmos* is a series of six books of graded piano music by what innovative Hungarian composer?
    a. Leoš Janáček
    b. Zoltán Kodály
    c. Béla Bartók
    d. Bedřich Smetana

66. What was the final book by James Fenimore Cooper in which the character Natty Bumppo appears?
    a. *The Pioneers*
    b. *The Last of the Mohicans*
    c. *The Pathfinder*
    d. *The Deerslayer*

67. Name the painter whose name is synonymous with Art Nouveau.
    a. Max Beckmann
    b. Andrea Mantegna
    c. Aubrey Beardsley
    d. Morris Louis

68. During Mozart's lifetime, who was the composer's most venomous rival?
    a. Haydn
    b. Salieri
    c. Vivaldi
    d. C.P.E. Bach

69. What do the initials stand for in e. e. cummings's name?
    a. Eliot Evermore
    b. everything elementary
    c. Edward Estlin
    d. easy ending

70. Giant lipsticks several stories high and stuffed drooping fans are the products of what modern artist?
    a. Claes Oldenburg
    b. Tony Smith
    c. Salvador Dali
    d. Red Grooms

71. What character in *The Nutcracker Suite* is characterized by the instrument called the celesta?
    a. The Nutcracker
    b. Clara
    c. The Sugar Plum Fairy
    d. The Prince

72. What American poet with a gift for definition wrote "Remorse is memory awake"?
    a. Anne Sexton
    b. Sylvia Plath
    c. Gertrude Stein
    d. Emily Dickinson

73. Matisse, Rouault, and Derain were called the Fauves, meaning what?
    a. Colors
    b. Rebels
    c. Abstract
    d. Wild beasts

74. What German composer was considered degenerate by the Nazis because he was married to a Jewish woman?
    a. Kurt Weill
    b. Gustav Mahler
    c. Paul Hindemith
    d. Arnold Schoenberg

75. What St. Louis-born poet, critic, and playwright became a British subject and a member of the Church of England?
    a. Ralph Waldo Emerson
    b. T. S. Eliot
    c. Eugene O'Neill
    d. Ezra Pound

76. In addition to the Sistine Chapel, many walls of the Vatican are decorated with frescoes by what immortal artist?
    a. Velázquez
    b. Raphael
    c. Van Eyck
    d. Ingres

77. In Menotti's opera *Amahl and the Night Visitors*, who are the night visitors?
    a. Soldiers
    b. Mediums
    c. The Three Wise Men
    d. Spirits from beyond

78. Why was Faulkner rejected by the army?
    a. He was overweight
    b. He was underweight
    c. He had poor eyesight
    d. He had epilepsy

79. Name the French cathedral most famous for its stained glass.
    a. Chartres
    b. Notre-Dame
    c. St. Maclou
    d. Amiens

80. What is the name of the lovely automaton in Offenbach's *Tales of Hoffmann*?
    a. Olympia
    b. Giulietta
    c. Stella
    d. Antonia

81. Which author created the character Sam Spade?
    a. John Steinbeck
    b. William Saroyan
    c. Mickey Spillane
    d. Dashiell Hammett

82. What Nazi leader was a ravenous collector of fine art?
    a. Goering
    b. Hitler
    c. Eichmann
    d. Speer

83. What composer had to learn to play the piano in secret because his father hated music?
    a. Brahms
    b. Bach
    c. Handel
    d. Beethoven

84. In *Moby-Dick*, what was Queequeg's foremost skill?
    a. Sailor
    b. Harpooner
    c. Scrivener
    d. Carpenter

85. The major endowment for the Museum of Modern Art in New York is from what source?
    a. Federal government
    b. J. P. Morgan estate
    c. New York State
    d. The Rockefellers

86. Name the composer of the *New World Symphony*.
    a. Bruckner
    b. Dvořák
    c. Holst
    d. Stravinsky

87. Cobweb, Moth, Mustardseed, and Peaseblossom appear in which of Shakespeare's comedies?
    a. *The Tempest*
    b. *Love's Labour's Lost*
    c. *A Midsummer Night's Dream*
    d. *Much Ado About Nothing*

88. What Italian city hosts an international art show and competition every year?
    a. Rome
    b. Milan
    c. Venice
    d. Naples

89. César Franck's only symphony is written in what key?
    a. D Minor
    b. C Major
    c. B Minor
    d. D Major

90. What prevented Odysseus's wife, Penelope, from completing the weaving of a shawl and thus having to choose a new husband?
    a. Pricks her finger
    b. Unravels the garment
    c. Runs out of thread
    d. Is bewitched

91. Leonardo Da Vinci's *Last Supper* is located in what city?
    a. Rome
    b. Florence
    c. Venice
    d. Milan

92. Grieg composed "Anitra's Dance" and other lovely melodies as incidental music to which work by Ibsen?
    a. *A Doll's House*
    b. *Rosmersholm*
    c. *Peer Gynt*
    d. *The Master Builder*

93. Who was the composer of "Onward, Christian Soldiers"?
    a. Handel
    b. Benjamin Britten
    c. Sir Arthur Sullivan
    d. Sir Thomas Beecham

94. What is the best-known panel in the Sistine Chapel?
    a. *Christ on the Cross*
    b. *The Expulsion from Paradise*
    c. *The Temptation of Eve*
    d. *The Creation of Adam*

95. The familiar "William Tell Overture," long identified with the Lone Ranger, is taken from an opera by what composer?
    a. Weber
    b. Rossini
    c. Nicolai
    d. Mozart

96. Which language ranks first in the number of people speaking it?
    a. English
    b. Russian
    c. Chinese
    d. French

97. The *Victory of Samothrace* is in what museum?
    a. Metropolitan Museum
    b. Louvre
    c. British Museum
    d. Smithsonian Institution

98. What Wagner opera takes place in Brittany and Cornwall?
    a. *Parsifal*
    b. *Tannhäuser*
    c. *Lohengrin*
    d. *Tristan und Isolde*

99. Who is the man who cuckolds the hero of Joyce's *Ulysses*?
    a. Blazes Boylan
    b. Buck Mulligan
    c. J. J. O'Molloy
    d. Stephen Spender

100. Who designed the topless bathing suit?
    a. Christian Dior
    b. Claude Montana
    c. Givenchy
    d. Rudi Gernreich

Answers

1. **C** Greek. He was born Domenikos Theotocopoulos in Crete around 1541, and later settled in Toledo, Spain.

2. **D** Eight years old. Mozart was a child prodigy unmatched in musical history.

3. **A** Hazel. He's a brave rabbit who leads his colony on a perilous journey to eventual safety in this novel by Richard Adams.

4. **D** *Time* magazine. In a 1964 article about a new fad in the art world, the magazine used the term to describe concentric lines to create an optical illusion.

5. **C** Johannes Brahms. He was also coincidentally born in the red-light district of Hamburg.

6. **B** Excalibur. As Arthur is dying, he commands Sir Bedivere to throw it into the water, where it is assumed that the Lady of the Lake catches it.

7. **C** Light and shade in painting. The term was first used in Renaissance painting.

8. **D** Chopin. He popularized this slowing down or speeding up of tempo for musical effect.

9. **B** Dylan Thomas. The poet's own alcoholic raging was as celebrated as his literary works.

10. **D** Henry Miller. His paintings, childlike and in vivid colors, are similar to those of Chagall.

11. **C** Napoleon. Beethoven became disillusioned with him when Napoleon declared himself Emperor and divorced himself from the common man.

12. **C** Thomas à Becket. He was murdered on December 29, 1170 by four knights of Henry II's court.

13. **B** Manet. Édouard Manet made a lifetime study of light and shadow in **paintings of people**.

14. **D** Wagner. He got no resistance from Cosima Liszt's husband because he was such an idolator of Wagner!

15. **C** Beans. He planted and tilled seven miles of bean rows.

16. **A** Toulouse-Lautrec. Handicapped for life due to a childhood accident that broke both his legs and left them stunted, the artist painted dancehall girls, musicians, and circus performers.

17. **B** Erik Satie. He was known for his bizarre embellishments and revolts against the conventions of composition.

18. **A** "Jabberwocky." The ballad is in Lewis Carroll's *Through the Looking Glass*.

19. **B** The 1913 New York Armory Show. Marcel Duchamp's *Nude Descending a Staircase* was greeted with public hostility and shock, as were all the great new painters of that day.

20. **A** Alexandre Dumas *fils*. He was the illegitimate son of Alexandre Dumas *père,* who wrote *The Count of Monte Cristo* and *The Three Musketeers*.

21. **D** Henry James. His *Portrait of a Lady*, which was written in 1881, is considered one of his finest works.

22. **C** Gesso. It's plaster of paris or gypsum with glue spread on canvas to prevent the paint from "bleeding" or spreading.

23. **B** *Swan Lake*. It flopped at its debut in 1876, but was successful in its 1895 revival.

24. **A** West Egg, Long Island. It was here Jay Gatsby built a shining palace across the waters from the home of lovely Daisy Buchanan.

25. **A** *Guernica*. It was Picasso's reaction to the Spanish Civil War. The painting has been returned to Spain.

26. **C** *Brandenburg Concertos*. They were dedicated to the Margrave of Brandenburg.

27. **D** They're possessed by spirits. It's considered one of the first modern psychological pieces of fiction.

28. **B** Leonardo da Vinci. He practiced dissection to understand animal and human anatomy.

29. **A** *Carmen*. It created a sensation with its innovative music and amoral story.

30. **D** Beatrix Potter. She wrote *The Tale of Peter Rabbit* and many other classic children's books.

31. **A** The clerestory. Such windows were widely used in medieval churches to illuminate a dark interior.

32. **B** Borodin. He often wondered if his career as a composer was worth the bother.

33. **C** Yes. This word begins and ends Molly Bloom's nonstop soliloquy that goes on for 24,000 words without a stitch of punctuation.

34. **A** An Early Christian church. Built under Justinian in A.D. 532, it did not become a mosque until the 15th century when the Turks conquered the city.

35. **C** The *Rhenish*. It was inspired by the Rhine River area of Germany.

36. **B** Cézanne. The artist was like a brother to Zola.

37. **B** Bernini. Famous for his painting, sculpture, and theater designs, he also designed the massive oval colonnade in front of the church.

38. **D** Bohemia. Smetana captured the flavor and spirit of his native land with such works as *The Bartered Bride*, one of the few true folk operas.

39. **B** Peter De Vries. The author is known for his biting satire.

40. **A** LeRoy Neiman. He gained pop culture fame for his sketches of basketball and football games.

41. **B** Ralph Vaughan Williams. He hadn't begun actively composing until his early thirties.

42. **C** Writes novels. Lessing's themes include Africa, Communism, women, and global catastrophe.

43. **A** Ballerinas. Although he did many pastels and sculptures, Degas is most famous for backstage and exercise portraits.

44. **B** Gustav Mahler. He also conducted an invisible orchestra with one finger in his final hours.

45. **B** Donald Barthelme. It was one of a collection of short stories in *Guilty Pleasures*.

46. **B** Picasso. She was forty years his junior, the sixth woman to live with him, and she bore him two children, Paloma and Claude.

47. **D** *Fidelio*. Written in 1803, it was originally titled *Leonore*. From this work sprang the well-known *Leonore Overtures*.

48. **B** Larry McMurtry. He also wrote the novel *Terms of Endearment*, which won the Best Picture Academy Award for 1983.

49. **D** History of the work since it left the artist's hand. It aids in checking the authenticity of the art work.

50. **B** *La Fanciulla del West*. Translated as "The Girl of the Golden West," it was an enormous success upon its debut in 1910, but is seldom revived now.

51. **C** The *Oresteia*. The trilogy consists of *Agamemnon*, *Choëphoroe*, and *Eumenides*.

52. **C** Flowers. The influence of her photographer husband, Alfred Stieglitz, is clear in her closeups of the inner folds of flowers.

53. **B** Haydn. He taught Beethoven when the latter was just in his early twenties.

54. **C** Rochester. The book was Charlotte Brontë's only truly successful novel.

55. **B** Buckminster Fuller. He created this dome of triangles, the legs of which were joined by spheres, as a living space. Fuller even envisioned a domed-over Manhattan Island.

56. **D** *Werther*. Written by Massenet and first performed in 1892, it was based on Goethe's novel *The Sorrows of Young Werther*.

57. **C** Lord Byron. His complete name was George Gordon Noel Byron—the sixth Baron Byron of Rochdale.

58. **C** Gilbert Stuart. Born in Rhode Island, Stuart lived in Boston and painted prominent citizens of his day.

59. **B**   Ravel. He created the *Concerto in D Major for Piano (Left Hand) and Orchestra* for one-armed pianist Paul Wittgenstein.

60. **C**   The Profane Host. Chaucer never completed his masterpiece of stories told during a pilgrimage.

61. **C**   Grant Wood. Often mistaken as a tribute to Middle America, it was actually Wood's satirical statement and lampoon of a social type.

62. **B**   *I Pagliacci*. This one-act masterwork by Ruggiero Leoncavallo has a main character, Canio, who's one of the most famous icons of opera.

63. **B**   Joseph Conrad. Polish born, he served in the French marine service at age seventeen and then in the English merchant service. In 1894 he turned to writing.

64. **B**   *Balzac*. Rodin's own photo-portrait was done by Edward Steichen.

65. **C**   Béla Bartók. His musical ideas are coincidentally expressed in these pieces.

66. **D**   *The Deerslayer*. The entire group of stories by Cooper was entitled *The Leatherstocking Tales*.

67. **C**   Beardsley. He was an illustrator best remembered for his drawings for Oscar Wilde's *Salome* in the 1890s.

68. **B**   Salieri. This composer sent cohorts to jeer at the performances of Mozart's work. His envy has been dramatized in the Broadway play *Amadeus*.

69. **C**   Edward Estlin. *The Enormous Room* is an exceptional prose account of cummings's World War I internment in France.

70. **A**   Claes Oldenburg. His giant objects—which include a huge hamburger—are done for open spaces.

71. **C**   The Sugar Plum Fairy. The character is evoked by the delicate chime-like sound of the celesta—an instrument Tchaikovsky discovered in Paris and kept secret lest other composers exploit it first.

72. **D**   Emily Dickinson. Although she composed over one thousand lyrics dealing with religion, love, nature, and death, her fame came posthumously.

73. **D**   Wild beasts. Their violent colors and distortions created a sensation and a critic dubbed the artists "wild beasts."

74. **C**   Paul Hindemith. He emigrated with his wife to the United States in the mid-1930s.

75. **B**   T. S. Eliot. The first two initials stand for Thomas Stearns.

76. **B**   Raphael. A contemporary of Michelangelo, he produced his most famous fresco, the *School of Athens*, as a group portrait of Greek philosophers.

77. **C**   The Three Wise Men. They have come searching for the newborn Christ.

78. **B**   He was underweight. The great writer was also only 5'5" tall.

79. **A**   Chartres. Considered a masterpiece of High Gothic style, the cathedral has windows that form translucent walls of color.

80. **A**   Olympia. The role of Olympia, along with those of the other three objects of Hoffmann's love, is usually sung by a single soprano.

81. **D**   Dashiell Hammett. Considered the original hard-boiled private eye, Spade was adapted by Hammett into a successful radio character.

82. **A**   Goering. He literally looted some of the great collections in Paris and even appropriated many fine works from the Louvre.

83. **C**   Handel. He covered the strings of his spinet with cloth and played surreptitiously in the attic.

84. **B**   Harpooner. He befriends Ishmael and endures many adventures in the hunt for the white whale.

85. **D**   The Rockefellers. The Rockefeller family was almost solely responsible for its original collection and building.

86. **B**   Antonin Dvořák. He composed the work while vacationing among fellow Bohemians in Spillville, Iowa and drew upon Negro folk melodies for his work.

87. **C**   *A Midsummer Night's Dream*. All of these characters wait upon Queen Titania.

88. **C**   Venice. The Venice Biennale attracts international artists who show and compete for prestigious awards.

89. **A** D Minor. This is how the symphony is commonly identified.

90. **B** Unravels the garment. She did this each night; it's a trick used in many myths and fairy tales by women who won't be hurried.

91. **D** Milan. In the church of Santa Maria delle Grazie, the fresco is on the only wall left standing after a World War II bombing raid.

92. **C** *Peer Gynt*. The story spawned Grieg's famous Suites No. 1 and 2.

93. **C** Sir Arthur Sullivan. He's much more famous for the comic operas he wrote in collaboration with Sir William Gilbert.

94. **D** *The Creation of Adam*. In this panel, God and Adam have their arms extended and their fingers are almost touching.

95. **B** Rossini. He wrote thirty-eight operas by the age of thirty-seven, but never wrote another opera for the remaining thirty-nine years of his life.

96. **C** Chinese. While Chinese is spoken by most of the earth's population, English is second in number of speakers, with Spanish and Russian third and fourth, respectively.

97. **B** The Louvre. Often called the greatest masterpiece of Greek sculpture, this marble piece is eight feet tall.

98. **D** *Tristan und Isolde*. It's based on an English legend as old as the legend of King Arthur.

99. **A** Blazes Boylan. This cocky, jaunty tenor is Molly Bloom's lover.

100. **D** Rudi Gernreich. Even in the way-out sixties, this design shocked many people when he started the fad.

SIX

Sports

1. What team did the legendary Red Auerbach coach?
   a. Detroit Lions
   b. Brooklyn Dodgers
   c. Boston Celtics
   d. Chicago Blackhawks

2. Name the first horse to win the Kentucky Derby.
   a. Aristides
   b. Eclipse
   c. Whirlaway
   d. Jimcrack

3. What lasts forty minutes?
   a. Football quarter
   b. Baseball inning
   c. Polo chukker
   d. College basketball game

4. Who was the first man to win both the Pentathlon and the Decathlon in the Olympics?
   a. Bob Mathias
   b. Jim Thorpe
   c. Rafer Johnson
   d. Bill Toomey

5. In what sport would a player get "banjoed?"
   a. Soccer
   b. Table tennis
   c. Diving
   d. Boxing

6. What sporting figure's original name is Richard Raskin?
   a. Yogi Berra
   b. Muhammed Ali
   c. Renée Richards
   d. Kareem Abdul-Jabbar

7. What U.S. President once coached the Stanford football team?
   a. Theodore Roosevelt
   b. Ronald Reagan
   c. Richard Nixon
   d. Herbert Hoover

8. When was the first recorded Olympics held?
   a. 492 B.C.
   b. 776 B.C.
   c. 381 B.C.
   d. A.D. 79

9. Who is the oldest man to have ever started in a major league baseball lineup?
   a. Ted Williams
   b. Satchel Paige
   c. Mickey Mantle
   d. Larry Harmon

10. What college football team has won the most Rose Bowls?
    a. Alabama
    b. Michigan
    c. UCLA
    d. USC

11. When were the last ancient Olympic Games held?
    a. A.D. 394
    b. 78 B.C.
    c. A.D. 66
    d. A.D. 100

12. What major league baseball player once ran the bases backwards?
    a. Yogi Berra
    b. Jim Piersall
    c. "Wrong Way" Corrigan
    d. Roger Maris

13. In what sport would you use a "skeg"?
    a. Surfing
    b. Archery
    c. Bowling
    d. Trap shooting

14. Who stole home more than anyone else in baseball?
    a. Lou Brock
    b. Jimmy Foxx
    c. Ty Cobb
    d. Hank Aaron

15. What athlete's former name was Lew Alcindor?
    a. Jamaal Wilkes
    b. Kareem Abdul-Jabbar
    c. Bronko Nagurski
    d. O. J. Simpson

16. What baseball player hit the most grand slams in his lifetime?
    a. Lou Gehrig
    b. Babe Ruth
    c. Joe DiMaggio
    d. Ted Williams

17. Where were the first Winter Olympics held?
    a. St. Moritz, Switzerland
    b. Lake Placid, New York
    c. Oslo, Norway
    d. Chamonix, France

18. Who said, "I guess I forgot to duck"?
    a. Joe Penner
    b. Gerald Ford
    c. Jack Dempsey
    d. Arnold Palmer

19. What baseball team had the "Gashouse Gang"?
    a. Brooklyn Dodgers
    b. Chicago White Sox
    c. Philadelphia Phillies
    d. St. Louis Cardinals

20. Who was known as the "Kansas Cyclone"?
    a. Dorothy Gale
    b. Dizzy Dean
    c. Craig Breedlove
    d. Dwight Eisenhower

21. How often were the ancient Olympic Games contested?
    a. Every year
    b. Every four years
    c. Every two years
    d. Every seven years

22. Who has hit the most home runs in a single World Series?
    a. Reggie Jackson
    b. Babe Ruth
    c. Roger Maris
    d. Johnny Bench

23. Who did Jake La Motta defeat for the Middleweight Championship in boxing in 1949?
    a. Rocky Graziano
    b. Marcel Cerdan
    c. Tony Zale
    d. Sugar Ray Robinson

24. Where were the first modern Olympics held?
    a. Athens
    b. Paris
    c. London
    d. St. Louis

25. What is the shortest of the Triple Crown races?
    a. Kentucky Derby
    b. Belmont Stakes
    c. Preakness Stakes
    d. All three are the same length

26. Who is the oldest boxer ever to win the Heavyweight Championship in boxing?
    a. Muhammad Ali
    b. Joe Walcott
    c. Jess Willard
    d. John L. Sullivan

27. When did the Americans first enter an "official" team in the Olympics?
    a. 1906
    b. 1896
    c. 1904
    d. 1912

28. What sport employs a cesta?
    a. Wind surfing
    b. Gymnastics
    c. Polo
    d. Jai alai

29. In what sport do you find the Wingate Trophy?
    a. Croquet
    b. Soccer
    c. Lacrosse
    d. Skiing

30. What team's colors are green, gold and white?
    a. Oakland A's
    b. Kansas City Chiefs
    c. San Diego Padres
    d. Minnesota Twins

31. What college did the first U.S. Olympic Gold Medalist attend?
    a. Yale
    b. Harvard
    c. Stanford
    d. William and Mary

32. What is the lightest class of professional boxer?
    a. Flyweight
    b. Bantamweight
    c. Featherweight
    d. Welterweight

33. Where does the Boston Marathon begin?
    a. Natick, Massachusetts
    b. Boston, Massachusetts

c. Hopkinton, Massachusetts
d. Springfield, Massachusetts

34. Who is the father of figure skating?
    a. Jackson Haines
    b. Dick Button
    c. Louis Rubinstein
    d. Norman N. Scott

35. What was the first modern Olympiad to allow women to compete?
    a. 1896 at Athens
    b. 1912 at Stockholm
    c. 1928 at Amsterdam
    d. 1900 at Paris

36. What athlete was known for his "Georgies"?
    a. Gorgeous George
    b. Evel Knievel
    c. George Willat
    d. George Steinbrenner

37. Who was known as the First Lady of Baseball?
    a. Marilyn Monroe
    b. Jolene Tulloch
    c. Laraine Day
    d. Eleanor Roosevelt

38. Who was the first man to sail solo around the world?
    a. Joshua Slocum
    b. Sir John Lipton
    c. Francis Chichester
    d. Pierre Lorillard, Jr.

39. Who was the first woman to attempt to swim the English Channel?
    a. Gertrude Ederle
    b. Florence Chadwick
    c. Annette Kellerman
    d. Eleanor Holm

40. What is Eddie Eagan's claim to fame in the Olympics?
    a. He won five gold medals in one day
    b. The only blind athlete to win a gold medal
    c. The oldest athlete to win a gold medal
    d. He won gold medals in both the summer and winter games

41. What is the oldest American college sport?
    a. Football
    b. Rowing
    c. Baseball
    d. Tennis

42. Who is the only player to win the tennis Grand Slam twice?
    a. Rod Laver

b. Maureen Connolly
c. Don Budge
d. Margaret Court Smith

43. Where was the first golf course in the United States?
    a. Newport, R.I.
    b. Brookline, Mass.
    c. Yonkers, N.Y.
    d. Augusta, Ga.

44. What sport is also known as "coursing"?
    a. Golf
    b. Hurdling
    c. Steeplechasing
    d. Dog racing

45. What century saw the first bicycle?
    a. Seventeenth century
    b. Eighteenth century
    c. Sixteenth century
    d. Nineteenth century

46. What horse was the first to win the Triple Crown?
    a. Whirlaway
    b. Man O' War
    c. Sir Barton
    d. Eclipse

47. Who is the youngest Olympic competitor of record?
    a. Sonja Henie
    b. Nadia Comaneci
    c. Olga Korbut
    d. Nellie Kim

48. Who was the first man to win golf's triple crown?
    a. Bobby Jones
    b. Sam Snead
    c. Arnold Palmer
    d. Ben Hogan

49. What is the oldest continuously held horse race in the world?
    a. Cesarewitch Handicap
    b. Camptown Race
    c. Newmarket Town Four Mile
    d. The Charles Town

50. Who is credited with the invention of basketball?
    a. James Naismith
    b. Abe Sapperstein
    c. Theodore Roosevelt
    d. William James

51. What was the first U.S. team in the National Hockey League?
    a. Detroit Redwings
    b. Boston Bruins
    c. New York Rangers
    d. Minnesota North Stars

52. Who pitched the only perfect game in the World Series?
   a. Don Larsen
   b. Don Drysdale
   c. Sandy Koufax
   d. Carl Yastrzemski

53. Who was known as the "California Comet" at the Olympics?
   a. Archie Hahn
   b. Bobby Joe Morrow
   c. Robert L. Hayes
   d. Charles Paddock

54. Who was baseball's player number 1/8?
   a. Steve Chandler
   b. Frank Saucier
   c. Eddie Gaedel
   d. Connie Mack

55. What event is held annually in Williamsport, Pennsylvania?
   a. All-Star Game
   b. Old Timers Game
   c. Farm League World Series
   d. Little League World Series

56. Who has the most Olympic gold medals?
   a. Eric Heiden
   b. Ray Ewry
   c. Mark Spitz
   d. Paavo Nurmi

57. Who was football's first black All-American?
   a. William H. Lewis
   b. W. T. S. Jackson
   c. Charles Follies
   d. Henry McDonald

58. Who was the first Rookie of the Year in baseball?
   a. Don Drysdale
   b. Mickey Mantle
   c. Stan Musial
   d. Jackie Robinson

59. What college dominated the first All-American team in 1889?
   a. Yale
   b. Princeton
   c. Columbia
   d. Harvard

60. With what team did Babe Ruth begin his career in baseball?
   a. Philadelphia Phillies
   b. St. Louis Cardinals
   c. Chicago Cubs
   d. Boston Red Sox

61. When was the first night game played in pro football?
   a. 1911
   b. 1902
   c. 1923
   d. 1934

62. Who was the first black player in major league baseball?
   a. Jackie Robinson
   b. Larry Doby
   c. Roy Campanella
   d. Moses Walker

63. What was the first Bowl game ever played?
   a. Rose Bowl
   b. Orange Bowl
   c. Sugar Bowl
   d. Cotton Bowl

64. Where was the first All-Star Baseball game played?
   a. Ebbets Field
   b. Yankee Stadium
   c. Comiskey Park
   d. Fenway Park

65. Who is the only NFL player to be named all-league in both offense and defense?
   a. Elroy Hirsch
   b. George Connor
   c. Roman Gabriel
   d. Bob Waterfield

66. Who is the "Joe" in the phrase, "Say it ain't so, Joe"?
   a. Joe DiMaggio
   b. Joe Garagiola
   c. Joe Kuehl
   d. Joe Jackson

67. Where was the Spaghetti Bowl played?
   a. Shea Stadium
   b. Florence, Italy
   c. Boston, Massachusetts
   d. It's fictitious

68. What TV star once played with the Dodgers and the Cubs?
   a. Chuck Connors
   b. John Davidson
   c. Michael Landon
   d. Bert Convy

69. Where was the first Super Bowl held?
   a. Green Bay
   b. Miami
   c. Los Angeles
   d. New Orleans

70. How many times have the Yankees won the World Series?
    a. 18
    b. 22
    c. 28
    d. 29

71. Who is the only player to win the Super Bowl Most Valuable Player Award twice?
    a. Joe Namath
    b. Terry Bradshaw
    c. O. J. Simpson
    d. Bart Starr

72. What athlete has won in both the World Series and the National Basketball Championships?
    a. Johnny Kuck
    b. Hank Bauer
    c. Gene Conley
    d. Joe Gordon

73. Which team has played in the most Super Bowls and never won?
    a. Washington Redskins
    b. Minnesota Vikings
    c. Los Angeles Rams
    d. Denver Broncos

74. Who is the only man in the halls of fame of both baseball and football?
    a. Frank Chance
    b. Cal Hubbard
    c. Ed Walsh
    d. Rick Waddell

75. Which Super Bowl had the lowest attendance?
    a. Super Bowl I
    b. Super Bowl III
    c. Super Bowl VII
    d. Super Bowl XIV

76. Who was the first baseball player to play all nine positions in one day?
    a. Jose Cardenal
    b. Stan Musial
    c. Roy Campanella
    d. Bert Campaneris

77. Who has had the longest playing career in football?
    a. Johnny Unitas
    b. Y. A. Tittle
    c. George Blanda
    d. Joe Perry

78. What baseball team featured player number 96?
    a. St. Louis Browns
    b. Boston Braves
    c. Washington Senators
    d. Detroit Tigers

79. Where was the first pro football game played?
    a. Latrobe, Pennsylvania
    b. Canton, Ohio
    c. Decatur, Illinois
    d. Croton-on-Hudson, New York

80. In the famous "Who's On First" comedy routine, who plays right field?
    a. Why
    b. I Don't Know
    c. Today
    d. No One

81. When was the first televised college football game played?
    a. 1929
    b. 1939
    c. 1940
    d. 1949

82. What player has hit the most home runs in one baseball park in one season?
    a. Babe Ruth
    b. Don Drysdale
    c. Hank Greenberg
    d. Roger Maris

83. Which team has won the most Super Bowls?
    a. Miami Dolphins
    b. Pittsburgh Steelers
    c. Dallas Cowboys
    d. Oakland Raiders

84. What is baseball player Roger Connor's claim to fame?
    a. First home run king
    b. First umpire
    c. First left-handed catcher
    d. Hit first grand slam

85. Who holds the record for the most passes completed in a single football game?
    a. Richard Todd
    b. Bart Starr
    c. Joe Namath
    d. Fran Tarkenton

86. Whose career ended May 30, 1935?
    a. Lou Gehrig
    b. Connie Mack
    c. Babe Ruth
    d. Ty Cobb

87. Who holds the record for the most points scored in a single pro football game?
    a. Ernie Nevers
    b. William Jones
    c. Gale Sayers
    d. Bob Waterfield

88. What was the first professional baseball team?
    a. New York Knickerbockers
    b. Boston Red Caps
    c. Cincinnati Red Stockings
    d. Philadelphia Athletics

89. Who has the lifetime record for the most touchdown passes?
    a. Y. A. Tittle
    b. Fran Tarkenton
    c. George Blanda
    d. Johnny Unitas

90. Who invented the baseball glove?
    a. Fred W. Thayer
    b. John Muir
    c. Walter Jackson
    d. Charles G. Waite

91. In which sport do you find the Benihana Grand Prix?
    a. Bicycling
    b. Power boat racing
    c. Formula I racing
    d. Motorcycle racing

92. What city hosts the Gator Bowl?
    a. Orlando
    b. Tampa
    c. Tallahassee
    d. Jacksonville

93. Who is the only player to win the Heisman Trophy twice?
    a. Glenn Davis
    b. Roger Staubach
    c. Archie Griffin
    d. Jim Plunkett

94. Which player had the longest hitting streak in the history of baseball?
    a. Mickey Mantle
    b. Joe DiMaggio
    c. Babe Ruth
    d. Ty Cobb

95. Which hockey team has won the most Stanley Cup competitions?
    a. Toronto Maple Leafs
    b. Boston Bruins
    c. Montreal Canadiens
    d. Detroit Red Wings

96. Who set the record of having been voted the National Basketball Association's Most Valuable Player for six playing seasons?
    a. Bob Cousy
    b. Jerry Lucas
    c. Kareem Abdul-Jabbar
    d. Wilt Chamberlain

97. In the Winter Olympics, the Biathlon comprises cross-country skiing and what other sport?
    a. Downhill skiing
    b. Rifle shooting
    c. Speed skating
    d. Bobsledding

98. Which National Hockey League player holds the record for the most Leading Scorer awards?
    a. Bobby Orr
    b. Doug Harvey
    c. Phil Esposito
    d. Guy Lafleur

99. Who was the first athlete since 1886 to win three events at the U.S. Track and Field Championships?
    a. Steve Scott
    b. Carl Lewis
    c. Doug Padilla
    d. David Patrick

100. What college football team is known as the "Nittany Lions"?
    a. Georgia Tech
    b. Penn State
    c. Ohio State
    d. Columbia

Answers

1. **C**   Boston Celtics. Whenever Auerbach felt a victory was assured, he lit up a cigar.

2. **A**   Aristides. It was May 17, 1875, and he was ridden by black jockey Oliver Lewis.

3. **D**   College basketball game. This is the official time and does not include time out. A pro game is forty-eight minutes.

4. **B**   Jim Thorpe. His medals were revoked when it was discovered he played semipro baseball while still in college, but were restored posthumously in 1982.

5. **A**   Soccer. It is the slang expression for a player who gets kicked in the groin.

6. **C**   Renée Richards. He was an eye surgeon and tennis pro who had a sex-change operation. She went on to coach Martina Navratilova.

7. **D**   Herbert Hoover. He was a student there at the time.

8. **B**   776 B.C. It is the first recorded Olympic Games; however, many historians believe there were others before that time.

9. **B**   Satchel Paige. He first began pitching in major league ball at age 42. He was 59 when he pitched for the Kansas City A's in 1965.

10. **D**   USC. It has won the game an incredible 17 times.

11. **A**   A.D. 394. The Roman Emperor Theodosius abolished the games as a public nuisance because of rioting brought on by arguments over professional versus amateur status, during the A.D. 392 games.

12. **C**   Jim Piersall. He did it to celebrate his 100th home run.

13. **A**   Surfing. It's the tailfin found on a surfboard.

14. **C**   Ty Cobb. He stole home 35 times in his 24-year career.

15. **B**   Kareem Abdul-Jabbar. A devout Moslem, he changed his name while he was in pro basketball sometime after graduating from UCLA.

16. **A**   Lou Gehrig. Known as the "Iron Horse," he did it 23 times between 1927 and 1939.

17. **D**   Chamonix, France. The International Olympic Committee set them up for the first time in 1924. At first, both games were to be sponsored by the same country but in 1928 the Netherlands had no place to hold the Winter Olympiad so it was held in Switzerland.

18. **C**   Jack Dempsey. It was his response to why he lost the heavyweight championship to Gene Tunney in 1926.

19. **D**   St. Louis Cardinals. The nickname for the powerful lineup of players they had in the early 1930s which included Pepper Martin, Leo Durocher and Dizzy Dean.

20. **D**   Dwight Eisenhower. It was his nickname when he played football at West Point.

21. **B**   Every four years. They ran uninterrupted for nearly 1200 years for a total of 292 Olympiads.

22. **A**   Reggie Jackson. He hit five of them as a Yankee in 1977 against the Dodgers.

23. **B**   Marcel Cerdan. The French boxer, who was Edith Piaf's lover, was killed in a plane crash later that year.

24. **A**   Athens. They were established in 1896 by the Frenchman, Baron Pierre de Coubertin.

25. **C**   Preakness Stakes. It is a mile and three sixteenths. The Derby is a mile and a quarter, and the Belmont Stakes is a mile and a half.

26. **B**   Joe Walcott. "Jersey" Joe was 37 when he defeated Ezzard Charles. Archie Moore, who fought Floyd Patterson at 42, was the oldest man to ever compete for the title.

27. **A** 1906. The team consisted of 35 members—all of them in uniforms to make it official. There was no official team at St. Louis in 1904.

28. **D** Jai alai. It is the wicker basket used to catch and throw the ball.

29. **D** Soccer. It was first given to the University of Maryland in 1936 for the best intercollegiate team in soccer.

30. **A** The Oakland A's. Officially the colors are kelly green, Fort Knox gold and wedding dress white.

31. **B** Harvard. He was James B. Connolly, and he won the first gold medal of the first modern Olympics in 1896. However, he had to quit Harvard in order to attend the games.

32. **A** Flyweight. This class is for boxers up to 112 pounds. Frankie Mason won the first title in 1910.

33. **C** Hopkinton, Massachusetts. It has been held annually on April 19 (Patriot's Day) since 1897.

34. **A** Jackson Haines. He was a former dancer and ballet instructor who thought up the idea of using music and modified ballet for the sport in the 1860s.

35. **D** 1900 in Paris. However, women were only allowed to compete in tennis and golf. They first competed in track and field events in 1928.

36. **A** Gorgeous George. They were his gold-plated bobby pins.

37. **C** Laraine Day. While she was married to Leo Durocher (1947–1960), she took an active interest in baseball.

38. **A** Joshua Slocum. It took him from April 25, 1895 until July 3, 1898, to sail 46,000 miles in a thirty-seven foot boat.

39. **C** Annette Kellerman. She was arrested in 1907 for being the first woman to wear a one-piece bathing suit. Her life was filmed as *Million Dollar Mermaid*.

40. **D** He won gold medals in both the summer and winter games. Eagan won a gold in light-heavyweight boxing in 1920 and took a gold on the four-man bobsled team in 1932.

41. **B** Rowing. The first competition was between Harvard and Yale on Lake Winnepesaukee in New Hampshire in 1852.

42. **A** Rod Laver. He won the U.S., French, Australian and Wimbledon championships.

43. **C** Yonkers, N.Y. It was laid out by Scotsman John Reid in 1888.

44. **D** Dog racing. It is the ancient name for the sport begun about 5000 B.C. and is still in commun use today.

45. **A** Seventeenth century. A frenchman named de Sivrac invented the first, but it could neither be pedaled nor steered.

46. **C** Sir Barton. It took forty-four years of Triple Crown competition before Sir Barton did it in 1919.

47. **A** Sonja Henie. She first competed in 1924 at age ten. In 1928, 1932 and 1936 she took the gold in figure skating.

48. **D** Ben Hogan. He did it in 1953 after recovering from a 1949 auto accident after which doctors said he would never walk again, let alone play golf.

49. **C** Newmarket Town Four Mile. It has been run annually since 1665. The first woman to win was Eileen Joel in 1925.

50. **A** James Naismith. He invented the game in 1891 as a means of having an indoor ball game to attract new members to using the YMCA.

51. **B** Boston Bruins. When the NHL was formed in 1917, it was comprised solely of Canadian teams.

52. **A** Don Larsen. The Yankee pitcher did it in game five of the 1956 Series against the Dodgers. It was the first time in 34 years that any major league player had pitched a perfect game.

53. **D** Charles Paddock. He won the 100-metres gold medal in 1920. He was portrayed in the film *Chariots of Fire* by Brad Davis.

54. **C** Eddie Gaedel. He was a midget who played in only one game for the St. Louis Browns in 1951.

55. **D** Little League World Series. It was first played August 21, 1947 when the Maynard Midgets beat ten other teams for the title.

56. **B** Ray Ewry. He won ten gold medals in four Olympics between 1900 and 1908. All the events he won are no longer competed in the Olympics.

57. **A** William H. Lewis. He was named All-American while playing for Harvard. Later, in 1911, he was the first black admitted to the American Bar Association.

58. **D** Jackie Robinson. He won it in 1947 when only one player in the major leagues was chosen. After 1949, one player was chosen from each league.

59. **B** Princeton. They had five players on that first team, including a quarterback with the unlikely name of Edgar Allan Poe.

60. **D** Boston Red Sox. The Yankee legend began his home run career by getting his first one off a Yankee pitcher on May 6, 1915.

61. **B** 1902. It was at Elmira, New York, and the winning team was the Philadelphia Athletics. The team was made of members of the baseball team of the same name because the coach of the baseball team, Connie Mack, owned the football team.

62. **D** Moses Walker. He played for a Toledo team in 1884 as a catcher.

63. **A** Rose Bowl. It was first played in 1902 and not again until 1916. It was not actually called the "Rose Bowl" until the stadium of that name was built in 1923.

64. **C** Comiskey Park. It was held July 6, 1933. Meant as a one-time only event, it proved so popular it has been played ever since.

65. **B** George Connor. This Chicago Bear player not only has this solo distinction, but he did it three years running: 1951, 1952 and 1953.

66. **D** Joe Jackson. "Shoeless" Joe was one of the players involved in the 1919 "Black Sox" scandal over throwing the World Series.

67. **B** Florence, Italy. It was held in 1942 between teams of servicemen on duty there during World War II.

68. **A** Chuck Connors. He played with the Dodgers in 1949 and with the Cubs in 1951.

69. **C** Los Angeles. It was January 15, 1967, and the Green Bay Packers beat the Kansas City Chiefs 35–10.

70. **B** 22. They have played in thirty-three series to date and account for 50 percent of all the American League victories.

71. **D** Bart Starr. He won it consecutively in 1967 and 1968 in the first two Super Bowls.

72. **C** Gene Conley. He played for the Milwaukee Braves when they took the Series in 1957, and then with the Celtics in 1959, 1960 and 1961 when they took the NBA.

73. **B** Minnesota Vikings. They played four times, 1970, 1974, 1975 and 1977.

74. **B** Cal Hubbard. He was a standout for nine years in the NFL and then he was an American League umpire for 16 years.

75. **A** Super Bowl I. Only 63,036 people watched Green Bay beat Kansas City at the Los Angeles Coliseum. It wasn't even called the Super Bowl; it was simply the World Championship.

76. **D** Bert Campaneris. It was done as a publicity stunt for Kansas City on September 8, 1965.

77. **C** George Blanda. He was a kicker and played for teams continuously from 1949 until 1975.

78. **B** Boston Braves. In 1947, pitcher Bill Voiselle was so honored since he was from the town of Ninety Six, South Carolina.

79. **A** Latrobe, Pennsylvania. John Brallier was paid $10 to play in the game, thus becoming the first professional player.

80. **D** No One. Literally, this is the only position omitted in the Abbott and Costello routine.

81. **B** 1939. It was between Fordham and Waynesburg State at Triboro Stadium in New York City.

82. **C** Hank Greenberg. This Detroit Tiger hit 39 of them in his home stadium in 1938.

83. **B** Pittsburgh Steelers. They have won four times: 1975, 1976, 1979 and 1980.

84. **D** Hit first grand slam. He did it September 10, 1881 and hit only one other home run that season.

85. **A** Richard Todd. This quarterback for the Jets achieved this record with 42 completed passes.

86. **C** Babe Ruth. He grounded out in his first at bat, then left the game and never played again.

87. **A** Ernie Nevers. He scored six touchdowns against the Chicago Bears on November 28, 1929 plus four conversions for a total of forty points, his victorious team's total score.

88. **C**   Cincinnati Red Stockings. In 1869, the huge sum of $1400 annually went to shortstop George Wright.

89. **B**   Fran Tarkenton. In sixteen years of playing, he completed 342 touchdown passes.

90. **D**   Charles G. Waite. For the first thirty years baseball was played bare-handed. The first gloves were unpadded leather. The first padded mit was for catchers in 1891.

91. **B**   Power boat racing. It was sponsored by the restaurant chain of the same name owned by Rocky Aoki who won it in 1982.

92. **D**   Jacksonville. The first Gator Bowl was played New Year's Day 1946 with Wake Forest beating South Carolina 26–14.

93. **C**   Archie Griffin. This Ohio State player won it as a Junior and then as a Senior in 1974 and 1975.

94. **B**   Joe DiMaggio. In 1941 he pounded 91 hits in 223 times at bat for an average of .408.

95. **C**   Montreal Canadiens. They have won twenty-two times.

96. **C**   Kareem Abdul-Jabbar. Starting in 1971 (when his name was Lew Alcindor), then in 1972, 1974, 1976, 1977, and lastly in 1980.

97. **B**   Rifle shooting. This relatively new event started in the 1960 Winter Olympics at Squaw Valley, California.

98. **C**   Phil Esposito. Playing for the Boston Bruins, he won for five seasons: 1969, 1971, 1972, 1973, 1974.

99. **B**   Carl Lewis. He won the long jump, the 100 meters and the 200 meters races.

100. **B**   Penn State. They won their first national championship when they defeated Georgia 27–23 in the 1983 Sugar Bowl.

Scoring

What Is Your T.I.Q.?

There are six chapters—which are six tests—in this book, each comprised of 100 questions. You can determine your T.I.Q. (Trivia Intelligence Quotient) in any one of the six general areas: General Information, Science, History, Entertainment, the Arts, Sports.

Each question answered correctly is worth one point. Enter the total points *per test* under the appropriate subject.

You'll improve your scores and retain more information by taking each of the six tests more than once. The graph enables you to keep a record of your improved T.I.Q.

In the last column, headed "Cum T.I.Q." (Cumulative Trivia Intelligence Quotient), enter the total of your test scores. The Cum T.I.Q. divided by six (the number of tests) is the overall average score for the six tests.

TRIVIA I.Q. SCORE

Test 1 General Information	Test 2 Science	Test 3 History	Test 4 Entertainment	Test 5 The Arts	Test 6 Sports	Total Score	Cum T.I.Q.

Number of correct answers	T.I.Q.	Translation
41–42	80	
43–44	82	
45–46	84	Low
47–48	86	Average
49–50	88	
51–52	90	
53–54	92	
55–56	94	
57–58	96	Average
59–60	98	
61–62	100	
63–64	102	
65–66	104	
67–68	106	Above
69–70	108	Average
71–72	110	
73–74	112	
75–76	114	
77–78	116	Bright/
79–80	118	Gifted
81–82	120	
83–84	122	
85–86	124	
87–88	126	Superior
89–90	128	
91–92	130	
93–94	132	
95–96	134	
97–98	136	Genius
99–100	136+	